D0573226

The Great Put On

SEW SOMETHING SMASHING!

LOIS ERICSON
LINDA WAKEFIELD
GUEST AUTHOR

Acknowledgements

Special thanks to those whose energies are part of this book: to Linda for her talent and technical knowledge, Diane for the direct connection & insight, Len for his editorial assistance, love & suppport. To Britt Densford who was always at the other end of the line to help me with my computer questions. To a very patient and talented photographer, David Browne and the lovely model, Amilie Cain. To Mary Jane Hensley, the Pfaff sewing expert who helped me get acquainted with my new machine. Special recognition to the Pfaff and Bernina companies for the professional loan machines ....what a treat to have top of the line sewing machines to make sewing an even greater joy. Last but certainly not least a very special thank you to my long time friend Bets Barnard, my editor, art assistant and mentor.Her expertise as an editor was invaluable, her honesty and assertiveness refreshing! Without her encouragement to push myself beyond my limits, I would never have dreamed of doing most of the drawings.

Copyright © 1992 by Lois Ericson
All rights reserved. No part of this
book may be reproduced in any
form without permission of author.
ISBN 0-911985-06-9
Printed in the USA

Dedication

To all who enjoy sewing ... no matter what level of expertise or appreciation. I commend you for pursuing your individuality thru sewing.

"WHEN YOU START WORKING....EVERYBODY IS IN YOUR STUDIO.... THE PAST, YOUR FRIENDS, YOUR ENEMIES, THE ART WORLD AND ABOVE ALL, YOUR OWN IDEAS.

BUT, AS YOU CONTINUE -- THEY START LEAVING, ONE BY ONE, AND YOU ARE LEFT COMPLETELY ALONE. THEN -- IF YOU'RE LUCKY, EVEN YOU...LEAVE."

JOHN CAGE, COMPOSER

■■ ■■

Contents

Preface

It has been said that everything has been done before and there are no new ideas. Looking at fashion may be like the changing designs in a kaleidoscope. Each season, as a turn of the kaleidoscope, the elements of style are rearranged like so many bits of glass. The familiar and exotic are repositioned into a new 'look'.

We are going to explore those elements. Join us and expand your creativity!

Linda Wakefield

Introduction

Why am I writing yet another book?

For me, a new book is always in progress -- either mentally or in reality. There is a natural progression, a design challenge to solve. I'm always searching for the unusual, one clue leads to another.

I love connecting with creative people who always surprise me with a new adaptation of my ideas. I like to think of my books as a bridge between the sew-er who wants to be more creative and the' product'. So I have written this book for you. Take what you wish of what is presented here and make it your own.

Lois Ericson

Design

Design

Can design be taught? Probably not...however as with most other skills, learning can take place provided that there is inspiration, contemplation, stimulation and experimentation.

Let's connect designing skills with our sewing projects. How do we get the ideas? For some it seems so effortless and unlimited. Early in my career, I was 'afraid' that I had used up my only good idea! Just the opposite is true ..the more ideas you get -- the more ideas you get. If there is a secret to coming up with innovative ideas, it starts with knowing how things work. It's easy to expand or change a part of the garment when you know construction fundamentals.

How to start? Where to begin? So many choices. Do I start with the fabric...the pattern...the technique...those wonderful antique buttons? Of course, these are all possibilities for beginnings. I usually find that I need to be focused on the general design idea. To help me zero in on a specific idea, I use the 'window' technique to isolate a design.

DESIGN, cont.

To make a design ' window', I use a 5x8 index card or other firm paper.
I draw and cut out the approximate shape of the garment to be made.
This makes the 'window' that I'll be looking thru. The 'window' could
also be in the shape of a belt, a collar, cuffs or any other segment.

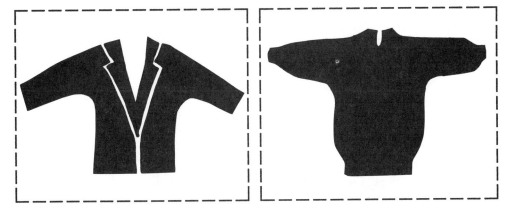

I place this cut-out 'window' over photographs or drawings in magazines or books. Images magically appear in the 'window'.   Ideas are
for the taking, all are one-of-a-kind. Most often they are asymme trical.
That is especially important, to me, because I rarely make anything
symmetrical. I want to have my designs balanced, but I find them more
interesting if the halves aren't equal or matching. The shapes that
appear in the 'window' are my inspirations. Try it, it's fun! It is a wonderful feeling to be original and work on your own ideas. Copying is simply
out of the question!

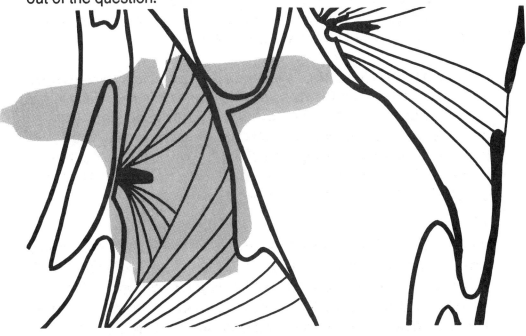

A printed fabric from Japan was photocopied. The shading film shows
one possible position for the jacket shape when placed on the print.

DESIGN, cont.

This is an interpretation of a painting. This process moves from inspiration, to isolating the design, to the finished jacket shown on the opposite page.

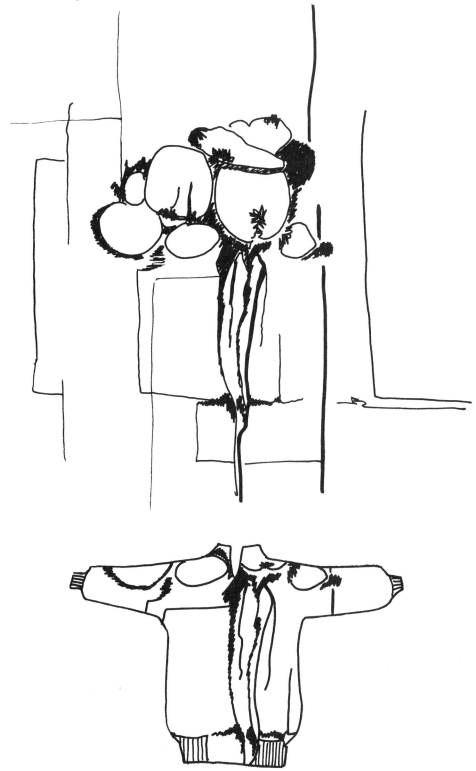

The rounded cut-out shapes are faced 'holes' with pleated insets. The fabric of the jacket is chenille velveteen with black cotton facings and painted cotton for the pleating. The front opening is slightly curved as the original drawing suggests.

DESIGN, cont.

When there is an intricate fabric design, consider choosing a very simply cut pattern. This makes it easier to construct and shows the fabric design.

Sometimes the 'window' placement offers a distinct suggestion as to the technique. The garment shaped cut-out just puts it in focus in relation to the project at hand. This inspiration was an African raffia mat that is a very graphic arrangement of stripes. So why not use striped fabric to 'get the effect'?

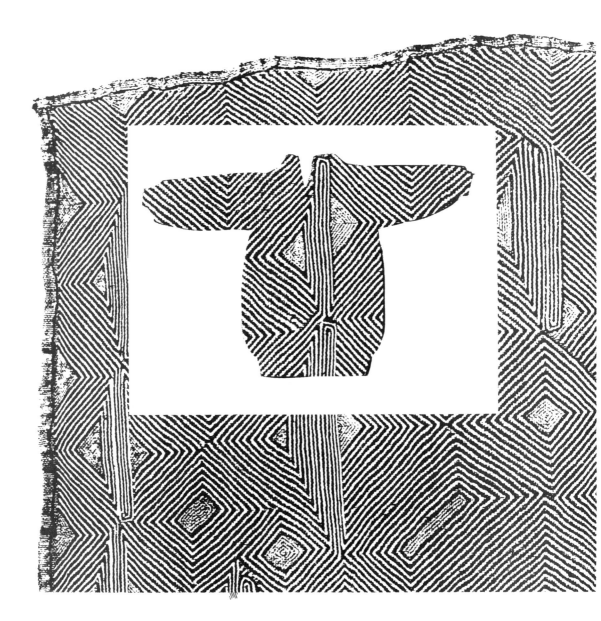

DESIGN, cont.

The techniques used were piecing to achieve the mitered look and faced shapes to finish the triangular and square holes. Sheer organza was chosen as the facing fabric for less bulk. The facings could have been a contrasting color if more attention needed to be on this detail. This baseball style jacket is made of charcoal and camel striped cotton. Brass buttons on the front and cuffs were a good color choice.

DESIGN, cont.

Another way of looking for design inspiration might be to choose a button with an interesting pattern. What does the pattern suggest to you? Look closely. Study it. The design could suggest strip piecing-- stripes with applique -- flat braid with sheer overlay -- trapunto with beading -- woven tubes.

Other possibilities for interpretation might be: rows and rows of stitching on textured fabric -- directional use of corduroy -- stitching a design in the grooves of the corduroy -- mitered stripes -- machine embroidery -- using wide stripes to create checks.

DESIGN, cont.

I do a lot of sketching in my notebook. I draw until I discover an exciting design that will work with my chosen pattern.   If the word 'drawing' inhibits you, keep in mind that no one will be looking at these drawings but you, they will not be exhibited for all to see. These are for your own information and inspiration. Once this technique becomes a part of your routine you will probably have more ideas than you will ever use. Drawing is a learned skill, we do get better as we practice. It is a great activity for fine tuning your awareness. Make note of those interesting or intriguing cuts or styling details, for all these ideas could be interpreted in future projects.

The question now becomes, "How do I interpret what I see into a sewing reality?" Do the images in the 'window' suggest some tech-niques to get you started?

> faced shapes
> pleating
> tucking
> layering
> piecing
> piping
> stitching
> applique
> beading

I find that once I get inspired, the actual work progresses smoothly. I don't usually make patterns, so I find a commercial one that is close in style to the one I want to make. I cut the main pieces from an under-lining fabric. After fitting and making any changes, this is the base of the garment. I cover the underlining with the fashion fabric that has been manipulated in some way, then finish as usual. Creating yardage is another method that I use. I then cut the pattern pieces using this fabric.

Suggestion: On your intended design make one decision and then act on it. It is easier to make one decision at a time. Of course, if you are good a visualizing, you will probably be able to 'see' it finished and will proceed toward that end.

Many people have asked me how to find their own 'style', my answer is: WORK! WORK! WORK! Your recognized 'signature' evolves gradually. When you have completed a large 'body of work' you will see your own personal *stamp* registered on the pieces.

DESIGN, cont.

The following is a *brief* list of potential inspiratations:

    Architectural:
        buildings
        roofs
        windows
        stairways
        gates
        bamboo fencing
        garden paths
        bridges

    Art:
        paintings
        drawings
        sculpture

    Textiles:
        ethnic motifs
        woven patterns
        textures

    Miscellaneous:
        mythological images
        calligraphy
        advertising
        graphics
        store catalogs
        tire treads
        containers

    Nature:
        shells
        rocks
        plowed fields
        bare trees
        leaves
        terraced gardens
        flower forms
        clouds
        fog, rain
        aerial photos
        waves

DESIGN, cont.

When I'm teaching, my two favorite words are Relationships & Simplify. Relationships are important in our lives, as we know, and also necessary in our work.

When planning your garment, place the fabrics, trims and buttons together. Do they relate? Is there some commonality? Maybe the rhinestone buttons are too dressy for the nubby texture of the fabric. When the garment is designed, the closure and/or other applied pieces need to be considered. These applications can be planned into the garment, not to be viewed as a possible afterthought but as a design feature. Consider if the piece to be used is compatible with your other choices. Can the original design idea work well with this added texture? Would it be better without it? Are the buttons or other closures going to enhance the total 'look'?

Keep in mind that this current project is not the only one you're ever going to make, so simplify! Consider choosing only one or two techniques. See how interesting it can be made by repeating and changing those few techniques. *Ideas*: change the proportion of the details, repeat the design motifs or limit your color palette. The calligraphy examples below illustrate that change of scale. Consider enlarging the motif, possibly using applique or faced shapes.... reducing the same design and stencilling it on a striped fabric.

So *try on* those two wonderful words Simplify & Relationships on your next garment...see how they *fit*.

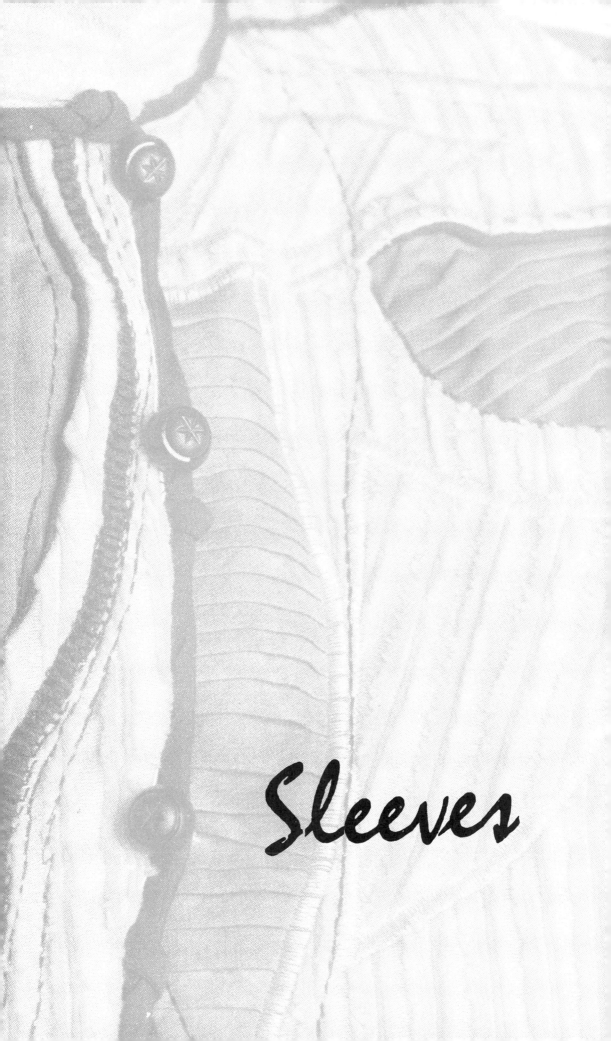

Sleeves

Sleeves

FULL, HUGE
NARROW
SHORT
LONG
KIMONO
DOLMAN
RAGLAN
TELESCOPING
ROLLED-UP
FLARED
GATHERED
PLEATED

Cuffs

WIDE
NARROW
RIBBED
PLEATED
TUCKED
FRENCH
REMOVABLE

Sleeves have all kinds of intriguing names -- leg-of-mutton, kimono, raglan, dolman. They can be full, gathered, pleated, flat, layered, flared, rolled-up or tight fitting. In other words just about any configuration or technique is possible.

Consider sleeves as a large *neutral* place on which to focus the design elements. This is an area of the garment that usually is out of range to our 'personal flaws' i.e. large hips, large bust, short neck or ? Very often this part of the garment is overlooked as a focal point. However it can be a most exciting one. If you need to change the basic sleeve pattern look in the Pattern chapter for assistance. We will be discussing ideas for making a unique garment merely by concentrating on the sleeves and cuffs.

COLLAGED OR PIECED SLEEVES

A collage is defined as an assembly of diverse fragments. Doesn't that just start the creative juices flowing? Pieces of various shapes and sizes fit together, like a puzzle. These pieces can be applied to an underlining that has been cut from the sleeve pattern. Place the pieces on that underlining. Finish the edges of each piece by overlapping seams, turning the raw edges under, satin stitching or covering the raw edges with bias strips.

If you prefer piecing, join multi-sized strips or pieces of fabric with narrow seams, taking care to keep the project flat. When you have created a piece large enough, cut out both sleeves.

This is a fairly spontaneous project. However, if you are more comfortable with planning your design, look back in the first chapter on design tips and get out the sketch pad.

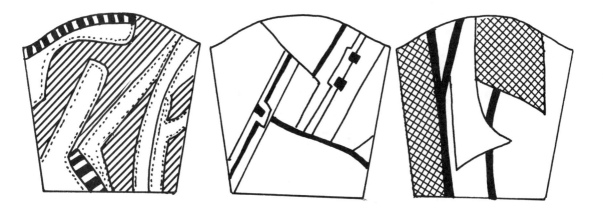

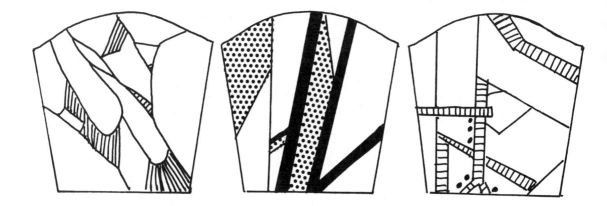

CONTRASTING SLEEVES

Any sleeve can be divided, several fabrics can be put together. This works especially well when the lower part is a ribbed knit, it brings the cuff area together, for an unusual fitted sleeve ending. Of course any fabric will work....maybe the sleeves aren't to be fitted at all. Applied facings is a technique that I use more than any other, so you may wish to add this to your list of special details. (see Techniques for facing instructions)

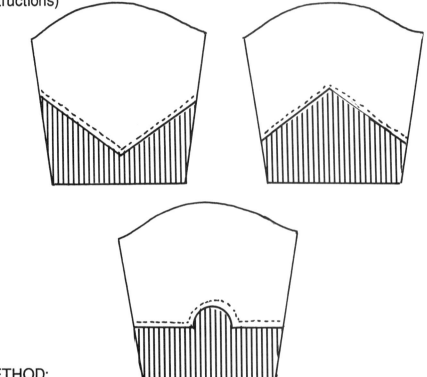

METHOD:

Start by drawing some sketches to see exactly what results you want on your sleeves. Then make a duplicate of your sleeve pattern. You may wish to make several patterns; experiment with various shapes. Consider designing the sleeves similar but not matching. They could be a positive/negative design.

Now that the decisions have been made and you have cut out the paper pattern, cut the fabric. Remember to add the seam allowances to those cut edges on the top piece of the sleeve. *Note:*The lower portion will simply be placed underneath to line up with the original sleeve pattern.

After the facings have been sewn to the top portion of the sleeve, trim, clip, turn & press. Slide the fabric of the lower portion underneath the upper part and top stitch in place. Finish the sleeve, as per pattern instructions.

ADD-ON SLEEVE

This is a fabulous sleeve that is applied to a finished garment and would make a vest (long or short) become a coat or jacket.

METHOD:

- hem 9" sides (this will remain open)
- sew 15" sides together (▼▼)
- finish cuff ends with a hem, by adding ribbing or gather or pleat onto matching fabric cuffs
- match center of 30" edge of sleeve to shoulder seam

Note: shoulder placement probably best half way between neck and shoulder -- your choice

The 24" length measurement, may need adjustment.

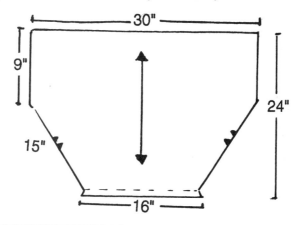

DOLMAN OR RAGLAN SLEEVES

Dolman or raglan sleeves usually have a seam from the neck to the wrist. This vertical seamline offers a great opportunity to create interest.

The first idea that comes to mind is to cover the seam with some embellishment ... possibly a braided or chained cording that could end by wrapping around the wrist to form a cuff.

Another possibility would be to insert piping in that long seam. The piping could be made in a matching or contrasting fabric...consider choosing an outsized cording, may be as large as 1/2" to 1". Near the ends where the piping is to attach to another seam, the *cording* needs to be trimmed at an angle to eliminate bulk. (see Techniques for piping instructions)

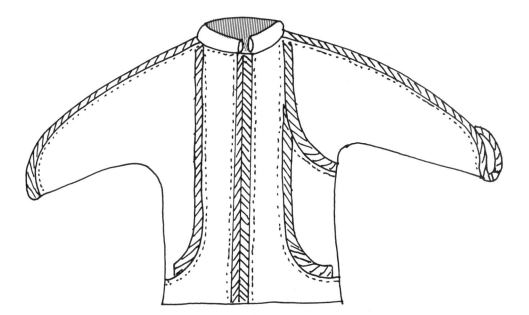

DOLMAN/RAGLAN cont.

This one was fun to figure out and even more fun to make. The concept is simple enough: the front half of the sleeve is cut longer than the back. On this kind of a cut, the pieces are very large, so it may not be possible to cut the added length onto the sleeves. On this garment, I added the 8"-10" for the insert. If your coat is a stripe or plaid consider cutting this added insert on the bias.

METHOD:

When cutting the front of coat add 8"-10" to the length of the sleeves. Make irregular sized pleats to use up those extra inches so it will match the back of the coat. Leave 3"-4"plain at the cuff area. Put the back and front together and stitch. Hem sleeve ends or add cuffs as per pattern. Nice idea to repeat on the collar.

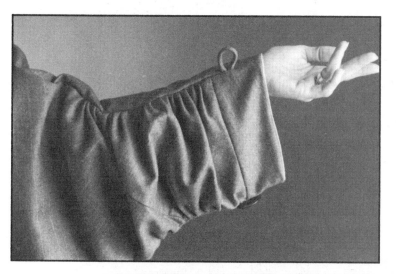

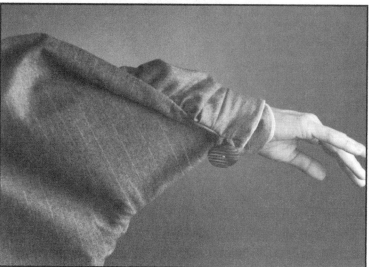

Start with this simple shape, and add heavily appliqued and embellished sleeves .... this will make an ordinary garment extraordinary! Consider using corduroy, the nap of this ribbed fabric could be cut to look like various shades (maybe you have done this inadvertantly on other occasions). All the applications are done when the sleeve is flat.

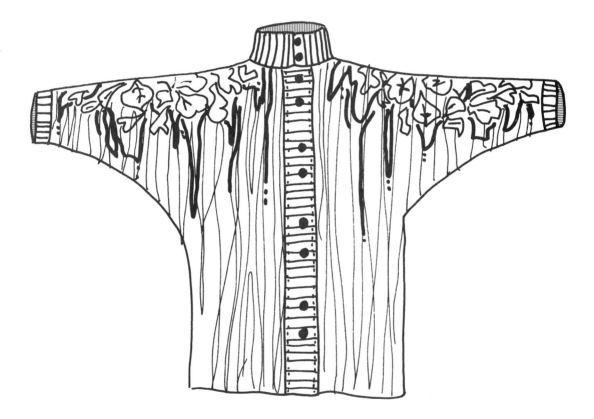

METHOD:

- cut pattern
- cut flower shapes or any other that you wish
- adhere shapes to shoulder/sleeve area with iron-on fabric adhesive
- stitch to garment
  This is an opportunity to 'play'. Consider creative stitching, with a twin needle or using contrasting thread .
- machine couch rat-tail or narrow ribbon for stems
- bead centers of flowers, apply beads randomly thru out
- finish garment as usual

DOLMAN/RAGLAN cont.

Inserting fabric shapes in the seams can be another detail to consider. The shapes could be rather small resembling a shoulder pad put on the outside... or very large extending from the neck to the wrist. Maybe the fabric that's textured in some way i.e. pleating or tunneling, could be used. I'm an advocate of using the shapes that are left-over after my garments are cut out. These negative shapes will be considered when making my decisions about the inserts.

METHOD:

Cut 2 pieces of fabric in the desired shape, plus 2 facings (can be a contrasting color). Place right sides together and stitch, leaving the side open that will be included in the shoulder seam. Trim, turn & press. Top stitch in place or leave the faced inserts loose.

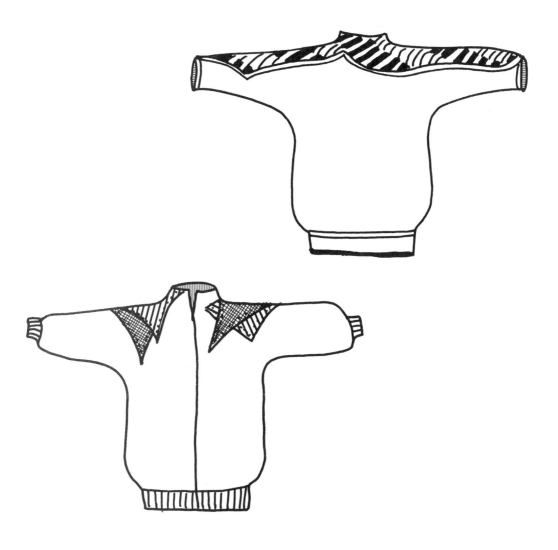

EXTRA LONG SLEEVES

What can be done with sleeves that are too long? Maybe this is a garment that you already have finished....or let's just do it on purpose. The look is usually casual so that makes it more fun to work on..in other words..this might not be a garment to hand down to future generations,

This drawstring idea can be used anywhere you need to shorten an area, i.e. the sides and/or back of a jacket....or a collar. However the sleeves are the most likely place to try it. The choice of drawstrings can be varied: shoelaces, ribbon, cording, leather strips are a few ideas.

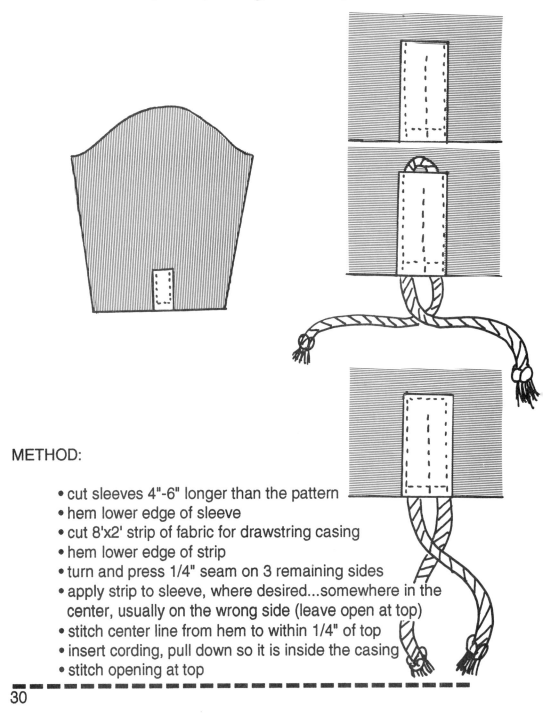

METHOD:

- cut sleeves 4"-6" longer than the pattern
- hem lower edge of sleeve
- cut 8'x2' strip of fabric for drawstring casing
- hem lower edge of strip
- turn and press 1/4" seam on 3 remaining sides
- apply strip to sleeve, where desired...somewhere in the center, usually on the wrong side (leave open at top)
- stitch center line from hem to within 1/4" of top
- insert cording, pull down so it is inside the casing
- stitch opening at top

EXTRA LONG SLEEVES cont.
This idea works well when used on a fitted knit sleeve.

METHOD:

- cut sleeves 8"-10" longer than pattern
- sew seams as per pattern and hem the lower edge
- if desired, insert elastic in the hem, also doubled ribbing may be used instead of a hem

To wear simply push up the sleeves, soft folds of fabric will encirlcle your arms.

Another option for sleeves that are longer than usual.

METHOD:

- cover narrow cording, about 30" for each sleeve
- cut sleeves 8"-10" longer than pattern
- measure and mark a point 5" and 10" from the top center of sleeve, sew small tabs of fabric (use piece of covered cording -- remove cord so it's flat)
- double the long piece of cording and pin the two ends onto the top center of sleeve -- aligned with the tabs
- sew sleeve with cording into armscye
- on the doubled end of cording, make a buttonloop by wrapping together with matching thread to fasten the loop
  Note: the loop will be the same size as the button, to be sewn in the appropriate place
- thread cording thru the two loops and button to draw up sleeve

KIMONO SLEEVE

A kimono sleeve is a straight tube of fabric, usually very wide so it is easy to wear over bulky things. However, it can get in the way. The following idea is one that makes this sleeve more practical...keeps it out of the way and yet is full and wide at the armscye.

The design of any kimono sleeve can be made more interesting by simply adding buttonloops in the underarm seam. Fold over a triangle and place buttons as seen on diagram below. To wear, just button, this creates a fold and a tapered sleeve.

A cuff can be added for special interest at the hem of the sleeve. Piping or other embellishments, such as antique buttons would make it very elegant.

I noticed this sleeve in a book of old Japanese prints. It was very wide with slits at intervals that are laced with beautiful cording. When the cording was drawn up tight, soft pleats resulted. When the lacing cord was wrapped around and fastened, a wonderful 'cuff' was created. It was great fun working out this design.

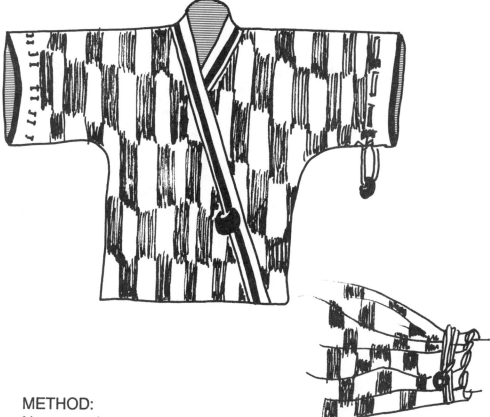

METHOD:
Note: cut sleeves 2" longer for ease
- garment is assembled
- make buttonholes, eyelets or apply grommets, as shown (make odd number of buttonholes so cord will start and end on the outside, placement -- 1 1/2" from outer edge)
- cut lacing cord 45",starting at underarm seam...thread cord all around ending at the underarm seam
- slide large bead onto cording, this will be the fastening device and also an ornament when sleeve is worn loose
- tie ends together in a square knot
- to wear -- pull unknotted end to tighten and create the pleats at the wrist (the knot will keep the cord from sliding thru all the holes)
- wrap the doubled cord around the wrist several times until the cord is used up and the bead is at the end.
- tuck the bead under several strands of the wrapped cording to fasten, adjust pleats if necessary

FLAT SLEEVE IDEAS

After the sleeves have been cut out, there is an opportunity to be very creative with this flat area. Painting, stencilling or appliqueing pieces of a print are possibilities. On this particular page the discussion will be about *placement.* Symmetry and balance are of prime importance.

The first example illustrates an example of symmetry. I applied a cut-out design and quilted around those shapes on the lower edge of the sleeve. The design was repeated on the bottom of the jacket.

Balance is achieved on the long coat even though the design is asymmetrical. The motif is placed on the cuff of the one sleeve and the shoulder area of the other sleeve.

TELESCOPING SLEEVES

To telescope means to have one cylinder slide thru another. This can happen when each cylinder is slightly smaller than the next. To adapt this to a sleeve idea, the pattern needs to be divided. Then when the extentions are sewn on, they will slide into the next larger section of the sleeve. *Note:* these extensions will be cut of some lining type fabric.

A. add 1/2 " seam allowance to cut top edge
B. add 1 1/2" seam allowance to bottom edge, add 1/2" seam to top edge
C. add 1 1/2" seam allowance to bottom edge

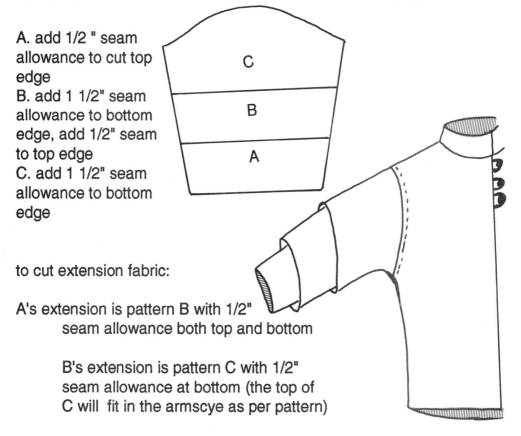

to cut extension fabric:

A's extension is pattern B with 1/2" seam allowance both top and bottom

B's extension is pattern C with 1/2" seam allowance at bottom (the top of C will fit in the armscye as per pattern)

METHOD:
- cut sleeves into three pieces, also cut extensions (lining)
- sew extension to the top of A
- sew side seams to form tube, finish seams by overlocking or binding
- narrow hem lower edge of B
- sew extension to top of B
- stitch sides together to form tube
- hem lower edge of C
- stitch sides to form tube
- slide tube A inside of B, overlapping about 1" pin then stitch in place
- stitch together where extension A meets top of pattern B
- slide C over B overlapping about 1", pin then stitch in place
- treat the top of sleeve as one (C and B extension) and insert in armscye

KNITTED SLEEVES

When a garment is quilted, or cut from corduroy or other heavier fabric, consider adding knitted sleeves for some added texture. The first association with this idea is handknitting... this sometimes will be intimidating. It is not impossible. I'm not an avid knitter but have made sleeves in this way on several occasions.

This jacket is a wool challis print that is quilted. The Art Deco era buttons, from the 30's, are green and black, with corded buttonloops hand sewn to the front edge. The pockets have flaps sewn to the lower edge of the yoke, the openings are on the sides of the inset pockets.

Machine stitch the sleeves in the armhole. I discovered that the sleeves seemed to stretch. I sewed a loop of elastic, slightly larger than the size of my wrist, to the wrong side of the knitted sleeve. The placement of the elastic is about 6-8" from the cuff. To wear, slip your hand thru the elastic as you put your arm in the sleeve.

The next idea that may surface is finding a heavy knit and ribbing to match the fabric of the jacket or coat that is in progress.

KNITTED SLEEVES, cont.

The third idea is also one that I would like to share with you.

Choose a man's sweater, either confiscated from your partner's wardrobe or purchased from your local second-hand store. Select a firm knit with nice tight ribbing. Cut off the sleeves and overlock to finish the cut edge. Insert in the armscye of your jacket or coat. The ribbing from the bottom of the sweater will finish the lower edge very nicely and relate to the over all design. Remember to serge the cut edge of the ribbing. If desired, the collar could be cut from the plain knit on the back of the sweater, or maybe it has a ribbed band at the neck that could be re-used. Thanks to Ronda Chaney from Redwood City, Ca. for this idea.

The fabric for this soft jacket is a woven chenille in shades of grey and camel. The zipper pulls are two rounded pods set in a metal band.

CUFFS & OTHER ENDINGS

Cuffs are a fold or band to finish the end of a sleeve. That is a very basic view of what could be the most interesting part of the sleeve .... the end. The lower end of your sleeve may be finished in a variety of ways. The hems could have elastic inserted, several rows, in fact -- maybe if it is decorative, it could be applied on top. Pleating or tunnelling could also bring the sleeve together to form a cuff. Various kinds of ties will be shown to give you ideas.

The cuffs could be lined with a splashy print, to turn back, if desired. The sleeve could have an elegant ending by applying trims of various kinds as a collage. The cuffs could be faced shapes applied in an unusual way. Let's explore some of the possibilities, starting with a very easy one.

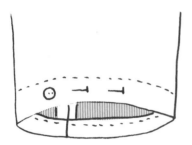 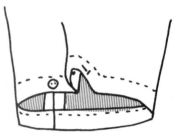

PLEATED OPENING:
- hem lower sleeve edge
- machine stitch two buttonholes about 1" apart horizontally on the hem
  Note: make sure they are exactly parallel and spaced so that when the fabric is folded vertically, they align
- sew button to the hem to form a comfortable closure
- form the pleat as you button the sleeve by aligning the two buttonholes and folding them to the button

The cuff on Linda's jacket is made of the top portion of a sock. This idea has great potential, since there are unliminted varieties of socks for men, women and children. Simply cut off the cuff where desired, apply as you would ribbing.

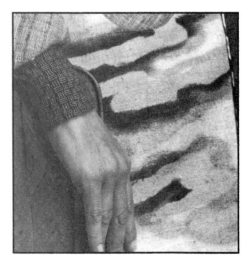

SLEEVE EXTENSION

Sometimes a sleeve needs to be lengthened or just have some added interest. It is very easy to do, just apply a faced piece to the end of a sleeve. It can be applied to a narrow or wide cut sleeve, trimmed with buttons or other decorative additions.

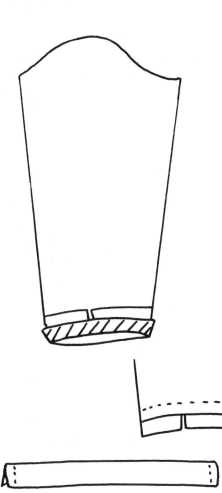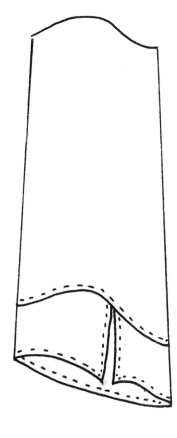

METHOD:

- measure lower end of sleeve
- cut strip of fabric to that measurement plus seam allowance
- for the width, twice the desired depth plus seam allowance
- cut & use interfacing if needed
- fold strip lengthwise, stitch ends
- trim seams, turn & press
- place cut edges of cuff to hem, pin
- cut a 2" wide bias strip and stitch onto cuff and hem, sewing thru all thicknesses, turn under bias, hand stitch in place

Note: if garment is lined the bias strip would be unnecessary

FACED ENDINGS

One easy way to finish the sleeve is to apply a facing to the hem. These can be various shapes, as shown below. On the rounded one with the two buttonholes, cuff links are used. The one with the triangular opening has a corded loop included in the seam of the facing. The straight slit has the buttonhole placed on the diagonal so when it is buttoned, it is parallel to the wrist.

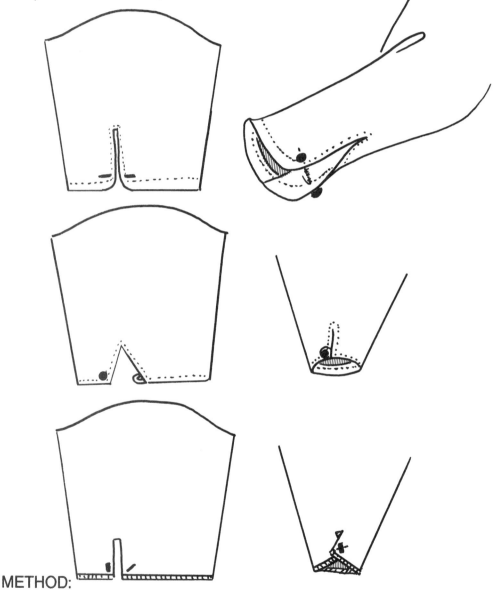

METHOD:

- mark the top end of slit and stay stitch
- cut facing for openings and hem on the top and two sides
- sew facing to sleeve
- *Note*:: if buttonloops are used, insert them with facing
- clip, trim, turn & press
- hem sleeve

NARROW HEM OPENING

A long sleeve, that is usually gathered or folded over to fit the cuff measurement, can be left smooth and the excess fabric may be viewed as a loop. This technique works best on coating, felted wool or melton...some fabric with 'body'.

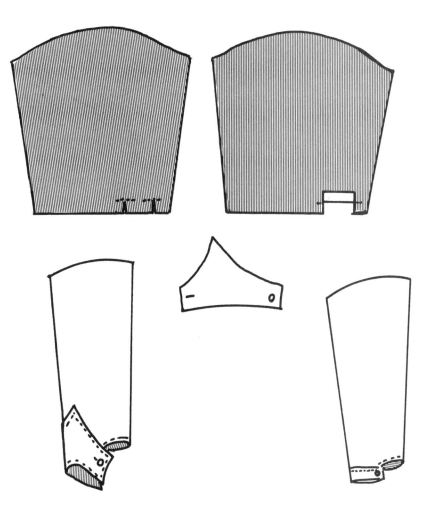

METHOD:

- to create a narrow hem opening, mark and reinforce the lower edge of sleeve in the area of the side front
  This will be the measurement that would be taken up by the pleats usually shown on the pattern.
- clip to the reinforcing stitching at the desired mark
- narrow hem the seam allowance and press
- interface and stitch cuff in the design of your choice
  apply as usual, topstitching the cuff in place, make button-hole and sew on button.

EXTENDED BAND

Instead of an applied band as the cuff, consider extending the side of the opening to form the band. This band will slide thru a faced hole and continue around the wrist to button. The band could be wide so it will create soft folds after it goes thru the hole. The sleeve might be narrow or wide, if it is wide the band would gather it in as it encircles the wrist.

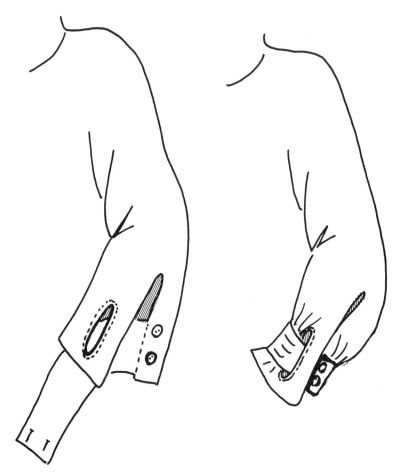

METHOD:

- cut sleeves out and mark the slit at the wrist
- cut two bands, twice as wide as required (plus seams)
- interface to the middle, lengthwise
- fold in half and stitch one short end and the long side
- trim, turn & press...topstitch if desired
- place finished band at back edge of slit and apply facing to the slit, this seam will include the unfinished end of band
- decide how long and what shape the faced hole, that the band slide thru, will be...and apply a facing..clip, trim, turn & press (if you need help with the facings, see Techniques)
- tack the facings, both on the hole and on the slit
- wrap the band around the wrist and mark button placement

TIES

On a coat or jacket the size of the ties are an important decision. If the garment is fairly bulky, or the cut is rather full, the ties should be wide to balance the 'look'. The finished ties might be 2" -3" wide, the length would be determined with a test strip. Attach the center of the finished tie at the seam of the sleeve. Sew on two carriers, these could be decorative as well as utilitarian... be creative. These carriers will keep ties in place. Tie square knot before putting on the coat, unless you have a 'dresser'.

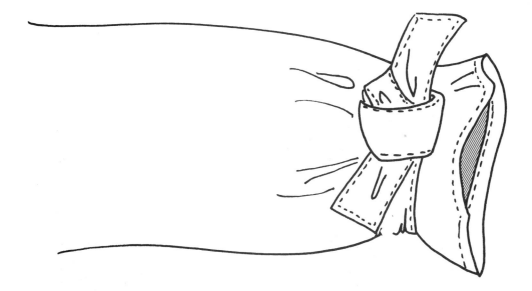

Another idea to gather a wide sleeve, is to attach narrow ties held in place by stitched small shapes of leather or Utrasuede.

CUFF FOR A TWO PART SLEEVE

Many blazer style jackets have two part sleeves, so this will be an opportunity to have some cuff area interest. Any sleeve can be divided, of course...just cut the pattern apart so the division lines up with the wrist bone. Remember to add seam allowances.

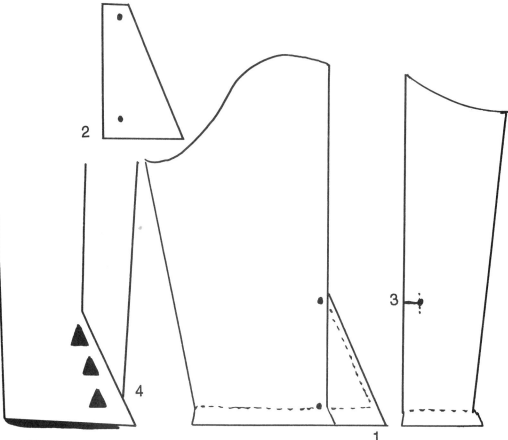

METHOD:

- about 6" from the hem on the front half of the pattern... add triangle (2) to the paper pattern on the outer edge of front sleeve then cut the sleeves (1)
- also cut facing to match, this could be in a contrasting fabric or a matching color with a different texture, since a little edge will show
- stay stitch back sleeve & clip, as shown, (3) turn under and stitch to hem sleeve opening
- sew facing piece to triangle on the two unfinished edges matching •'s
- clip & trim, then turn & press
- sew sleeve seams together to the •'s
- make buttonholes, or simply sew buttons thru all layers (4) *Note:* a nice relationship to the triangle would be to have a similar shape button

PLEATED INSERTS

In this divided sleeve there is a pleated insert. Pleated fabric is sometimes difficult to find, so you may wish to pleat it yourself using a cloth pleater. (See supply list.) Often it is easier to pleat the fabric and then cut the sleeves as per pattern. This idea can apply to tucks, smocking or other manipulating techniques as well. This approach allows more spontaneity in the construction than if the pattern was designed with the pleats. Consider pleating one sleeve horizontally and one vertically.

METHOD:

To insert a 3" band, cut 2 1/2" from the center of the sleeve. If there is also to be piping in the seams, apply that now. Stitch the pleated band to the piped (or plain) seams. Down the center of the pleated band, you may wish to stitch a row of decorative stitches. Another option is to turn the center of the pleats back and stitch. When the band is inserted, finish the sleeve as per pattern directions.

REMOVABLE CUFFS

What a great concept, looks like a bracelet...in fact that is where I got the idea. One could make several pair for one garment, to change the 'look'...from casual -- made of wide unusual elastic... to dressy -- made of elegant fabrics with fancy buttons and trims. They can be any width and shape. I always favor using scrap pieces that are already cut and applying facings to them. The cuff from the pattern can be used as the starting point. If they are wide, shaping them to fit your arm might be advantageous. Most all, except the elastic ones, need interfacing. Velcro or other similar fastening materials are useful. Buttons and buttonloops are always effective. These cuffs look especially nice when worn with soft pleated or loose sleeves. The cuffs should be quite snug to keep the pleats in place, so plan accordingly.

unusual elastics

METHOD:

- cut 4 cuffs from pattern, if you are designing these and need assistance, check Pattern chapter
- stitch trims or braids onto the cuffs in a pleasing design
  Note: if buttonloops are to be used insert now
- stitch facing or lining to the cuff, right sides together
- trim, turn & press....hand tack the facing in place
- add beads, decorative or utilitarian buttons
- if machine made buttonholes are part of the design, make them in appropriate places

REMOVABLE CUFFS, cont.

Collars

Collars

WIDE
NARROW
STIFF
SOFT
DRAPED
STAND-UP
FLAT
NOTCHED
REMOVABLE
TURTLENECK
RIBBED
PETAL-LIKE
SHAWL
TIES
HOOD
MANDARIN
TROMPE L'OEIL
OR NONE

The collar frames the face. It may provide warmth or camouflage neckline faults. Necklines and collar provide a wide range of design opportunities. They can start where they are supposed to and end wherever you wish, i.e. a collar that becomes a long scarf that can wrap around the neck and cascade down the back.

Reminder: since we are not making the patterns, the original pieces and shapes still have to connect with other sections as per pattern. So whatever changes that are made on the pattern to enhance the design, cannot be on connecting seams. The outer edges are the ones that we are changing in such a carefree manner, i.e. the outer edges of a collar or the lower edges of the sleeves or cuffs.

Some general ideas might be a double collar, asymetrical notches on a shawl collar or the collar on one side, leaving a plain 'V' on the other side. There can be stretchy ribbing, small ties or collars so large they become hoods. What makes a collar hold its shape? In addition to interfacing; quilting and/or rows of stitching would also make it firm.

Before getting too outrageous you may wish to consider your size, shape, and figure type. Is the proposed change going to be flattering? Maybe the collar is too wide, so you may wish to cut out an approximate collar of muslin to assess the look in your full length mirror.

NOTCHED COLLARS

A notched collar is exactly that...a collar with a notch engineered into it. Generally it is a collar that is constructed of two pieces to each side, plus the facing or undercollar. The discussion on these pages will be ways to change that basic collar design.

Think about changing the proportion of each of the pieces, without altering the basic cut of the collar. Each of the following drawings show ideas for minimal changes. Since the basic pattern has not been changed, it might be fun to choose one of these the next time you make a blazer-type jacket.

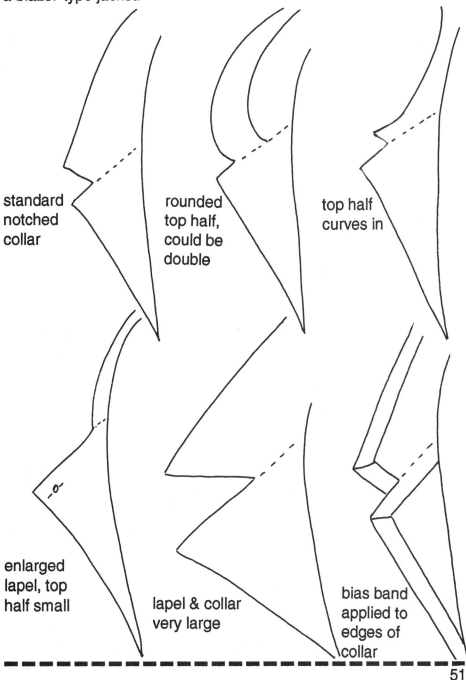

standard notched collar

rounded top half, could be double

top half curves in

enlarged lapel, top half small

lapel & collar very large

bias band applied to edges of collar

SHAWL COLLAR

A shawl collar is a rolled collar and lapel in one piece that curves from the back of the neck down to the front closure of a single or double breasted garment.

There are many possibilities to vary this simple neckline.
- changing the configuration of the outer edge by notching
- changing the size from narrow to wide
- making it asymmetrical, one side very long &/or wide, the other side smaller and shorter
- by dividing it in two, horizontally
- by placing 2 collars on top of each other

Changes are always easiest when you start with a pattern that is close to the desired result. This first example is an easy one. The outer edges of the collar have a little notch sewn in as the facing is applied, so when it is turned to the right side it looks very similar to a notched collar that is cut in several pieces.

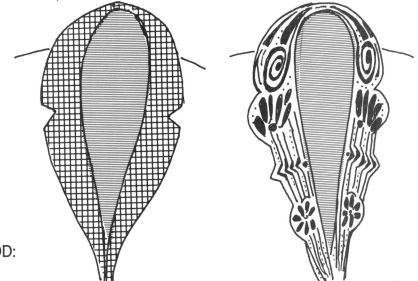

METHOD:
- cut out collar and interfacing as per pattern
- decide where the notches are going to be sewn
  Suggestion: make a notch mark on the interfacing with a sewing pen and put the collar around your neck to check placement
- baste interfacing to one piece of the collar
- pin collar pieces, right sides together
- as the outer seam is sewn, simply stitch the notch in.
- clip and trim seams, turn & press
- apply collar as the pattern suggests

Note :This technique could apply to any shape. Consider applying a geometric print to the collar pieces, then use the outer edges of the print shapes as the stitching guide. Continue as above.

SHAWL COLLAR cont.

A shawl collar can easily be divided horizontally. This creates more interest by cutting the pieces from two different fabrics, i.e. the lower 2/3 rds of the main fabric of the garment and the top 1/3rd a ribbed knit. Another idea for the top section would be to add 6"-8" to the top section and gather the edges before sewing sections together, remember to add the seam allowances to the cut edges.

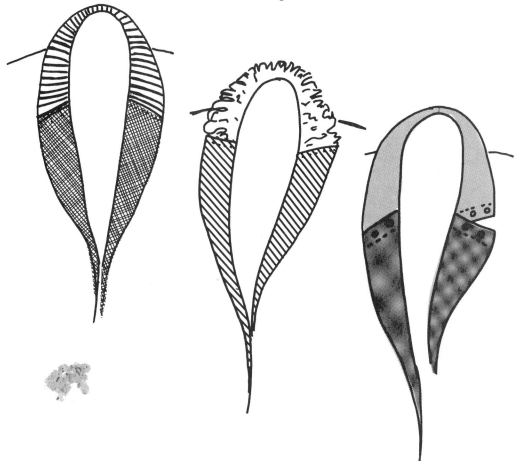

One of my favorite division ideas, for this style of of collar, is the third example above. When the collar is snapped together it looks like a shawl, but when it is open, it looks like a notched collar.

METHOD:

- divide the collar pattern into two pieces, about 1/3 and 2/3
- add seam allowances plus 1" at the division
- cut interfacing and apply to collar pieces
- pin collar pieces, right sides together - stitch, trim, turn, press
- there are now, 4 pieces with finished outer edges
- overlap the pieces at the division line, as shown
- apply two gripper snaps to opening
- finish collar as per pattern instructions

EXAGGERATED COLLARS, cont.

The general shape and size of the collar on this coat offers ample space to create a special design. Architectural forms are of interest to me, so I applied some building shapes on the collar. On the main body of this green wool coat, I stitched the shadows that the buildings cast on the ground. Faced shapes in a camel and black print were applied and stitching was used to accentuate the shapes.

EXAGGERATED COLLARS

The word 'wide' or 'huge' usually comes to mind when thinking of the word "exaggerated", so let's start with that concept. What happens when a collar is cut very wide? Sometimes folds or creases in the fabric occur, especially if the fabric is soft and pliable. Sometimes the collar extends past the confines of the collar area. I like the idea of a collar starting where it is 'supposed' to and ending differently. Unpredictable!

The collar on this elegant jacket is very large on one side, with piping inserted in the seams and just a plain 'V' on the opposite side. Nice contrast on this jacket by Linda.

'V' NECKLINE

This plain neckline can easily be changed by adding a band of fabric. This band could be pleated or cut on the bias and gathered, so it would stand-up. Consider 2"-3" for the finished width. Apply to neck edge and finish with a bias strip.

The band could also be a plain strip of fabric interfaced to the center.Fold and stitch the narrow ends. Trim, turn & press. Apply to neckline, stitching right sides together...leaving the underside of the band free to turn and finish by hand.

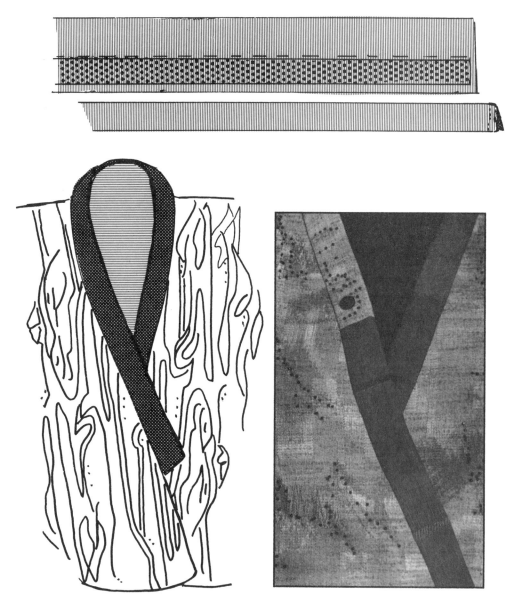

Note:: The two ideas shown here, wrinkled/stitched and beading, are both explained in the Techniques chapter.

MANDARIN COLLARS

A Mandarin collar is usually thought of in conjuction with Oriental garments. It is a firm stand-up band that opens in the middle. (A) It could be very elegantly embellished with embroidery, braid or other trims. (B) It could be removable. Finish the collar completely and attach button-loops to the bottom edge....sew buttons to the neck edge of a finished jacket that has a plain round neck. (C) It might be cut very wide, 8"-10" then pleated or shirred to condense. Insert buttonloops (see Closures) at the edge of the center front and many small ball buttons.

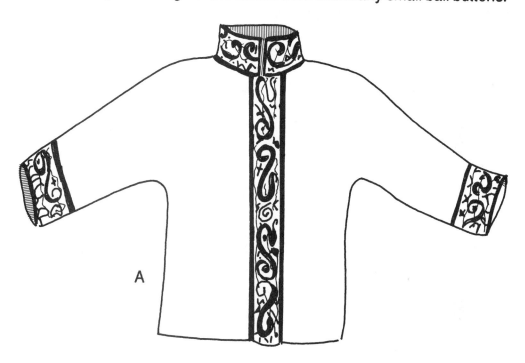

A

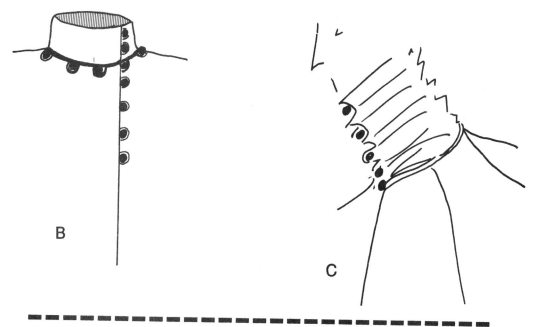

B

C

MOCK COLLARS

Trompe l'oeil
What a fancy name for something that is not what it appears! Collars (cuffs, too) would be the perfect place to use this idea. Choose a pattern that has a plain 'V' neckline. Pieces of fabric are cut to resemble the collar, facing pieces are applied so that each section is a finished unit except at the neck edge. Use interfacing if needed.

Pin the collar pieces to the garment approximately where a collar might be and stitch the pieces in place. Finish the cut edges with the facings that are in the pattern.

Another way to use this technique is to apply the faced pieces with a bias band at the very edge and leave the faced shapes loose. That is, only stitched at the neck edge with the bias strips. Cut the bias strips about 4" wide. Fold in half, pin doubled, covering the cut edges of the faced shapes and the neckline on the garment as well. Stitch, then trim and clip, if necessary, and fold bias over to finish seams. Hand tack in place.

MOCK COLLARS, cont.

Start with a' V 'neckline pattern and cut out some shapes, any shapes you wish. A few suggestions are drawn below, so play with those or add your own ideas. Cut the samples out of paper or fabric and try them on for size and proportion. Sometime the top of the shape is included in the shoulder seam.

The edges will be finished with a corresponding piece that could be matching or contrasting fabric. The open side of that faced piece will be the edge that connects with the neckline seam. This neck edge will be finished with the facing that is in your original pattern.

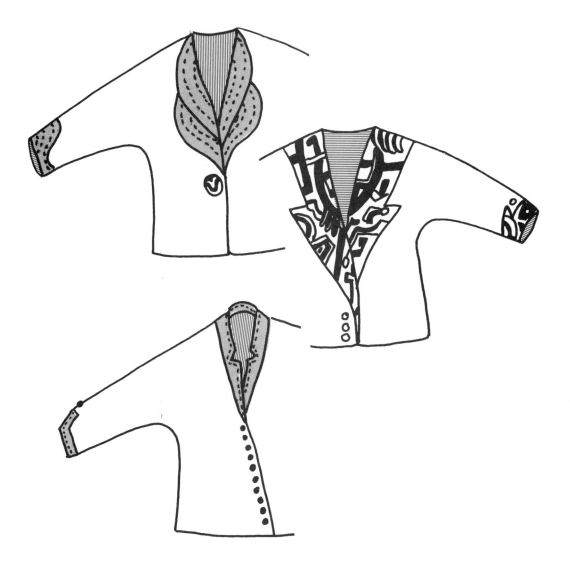

Pockets

Pockets

CONCEALED
OBVIOUS
HUGE
SMALL
IN SEAM
PATCH
WITH FLAPS
BUTTONHOLE STYLE
SLASH
MULTIPLES
LAYERS
SHAPED

A pocket is a shaped piece of fabric attached inside or outside a garment. Most everyone enjoys having pockets in their clothes. In fact, the first automatic move is to slide one's hands into that cozy space on a jacket or coat. Pockets can be any size from very small, so it is only decorative, to very large so it is only a handwarming cavity. In the case of a commercial pattern, the detailing will be determined by the designer and/or pattern drafter, it will usually look like this ▢ for a patch pocket or it might have rounded corners.

The other two options are welt ▰ or in-seam. ‖

Since you are the designer, the pockets could be the shape of your choice. Very often I use the left over scraps...whatever shape they may be and face them with a contrasting fabric. The placement of the pockets is also arbitrary, as long as they are accessible. You may put them wherever you choose. Maybe it could be very long and start at the shoulder seam or have several layers with various compartments.

If you are a frequent traveller consider including hidden pockets in the design of a travel garment for valuables. This may also eliminate the need for a purse which can free your arms for more important things -- like SHOPPING.

WELT POCKETS

Welt pockets are details that give your garment a professional look. If you have been intimidated by the application of welt pockets, this method may alleviate your fears.

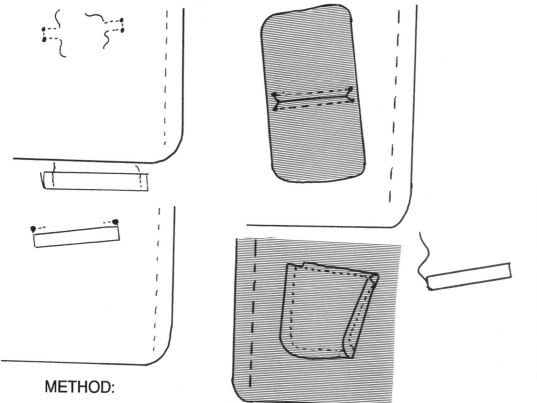

METHOD:

- reinforce front of garment along stitching line, see diagram, pivoting at ● as shown -- use small stitches
- cut welt,7" x 2 1/2" on the bias, fold welt in half, right sides together, stitch each end, turn & press (interface if necessary)
- baste welt to front, placing seamline of welt along lower stitching line, between ●'s. *Note*: seams to be included into pocket will be 1/4"
- cut pocket 7"x12" , the reinforcing line will be at the 6 1/2" and the 5 1/2 " measurement on the pocket
- mark reinforcing lines on pocket, the same as on the front of garment
- stitch along the lines, pivoting at ●'s
- placing the longer end (6 1/2") of the pocket at the top, pin pocket to front, matching the reinforcing stitching lines.
- stitch then slash between stitching, clipping diagonally to ●'s
- turn pocket to inside, stitch pocket edges together catching the triangular ends
- press welt up to cover the opening and slip stitch the ends of welt in place

PATCH POCKETS

One of the easiest pockets to make and apply is a patch pocket. These are sometimes referred to as 'Pot Holder' pockets. These pockets could be very plain and are on the commercial patterns. However, these could be: quilted, beaded, pleated to expand, banded at the top with contrasting fabric, unusual shapes, made with ribbing, cut full then finished with casing & elastic.

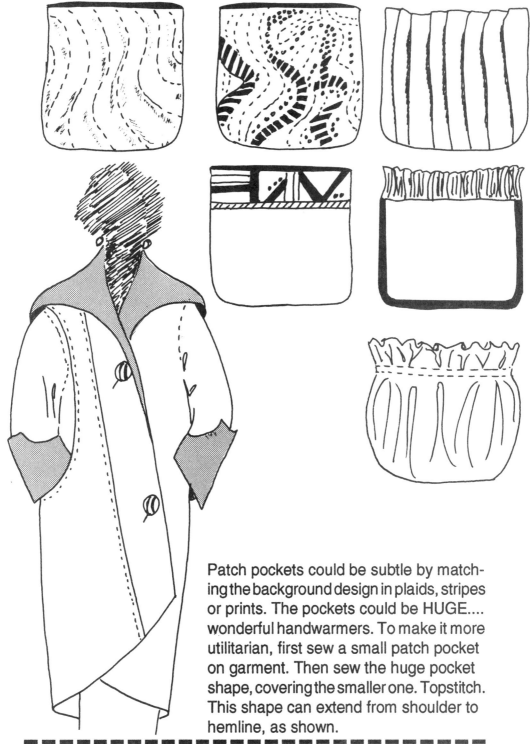

Patch pockets could be subtle by matching the background design in plaids, stripes or prints. The pockets could be HUGE.... wonderful handwarmers. To make it more utilitarian, first sew a small patch pocket on garment. Then sew the huge pocket shape, covering the smaller one. Topstitch. This shape can extend from shoulder to hemline, as shown.

PATCH POCKETS cont.

The front section of this pocket is faced with a contrasting fabric. This creates a lapel-like effect when the center sections fold back. The pocket is then stitched to a backing shape.

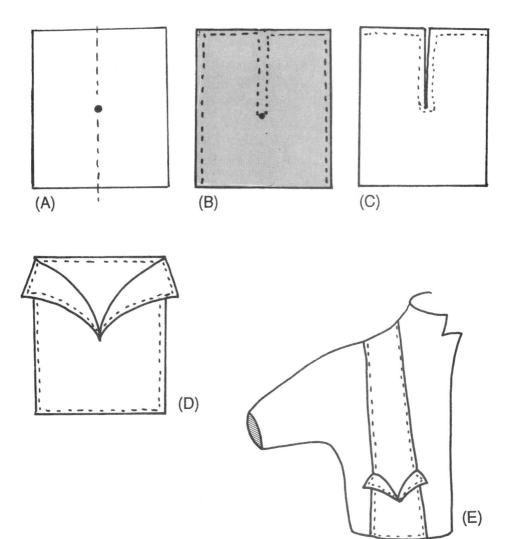

(A) (B) (C)

(D)

(E)

METHOD:

- cut pocket shape and facing 1" wider than finished width (A)
- with right sides together, stitch facing to pocket shape to the mark in the middle of the pocket (B)
- trim, turn & press (C)
- this front section of the pocket is now ready to apply to the back section of the patch pocket (D)
  Note: this back section could be about the same size as the front or extend to the shoulder line. (E)

PATCH POCKETS cont.

Why not include a zipper in the construction of the patch pocket? For an easy insertion consider the following methods. The first idea would be to add 1" to the size of the pocket, so it could be cut and seams could be added at the location of the zipper placement.

METHOD: A

- cut pocket with added 1" to length
- cut pocket apart near the top to make seam for zipper application
- sew each end of seam, leaving space in center for zipper
- press seam open and sew in zipper by machine or by hand
- press pocket seams under, in preparation for stitching onto garment. ...if lining is desired apply now , stitch, trim & turn
  Note: the lining makes the 'back' of the pocket or pouch
- pin pocket onto garment, topstitch

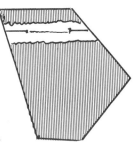 

METHOD: B

- cut pocket
- mark rectangular slit for zipper placement
- cut matching facing from lining fabric
- right sides together, sew facing, as shown, to pocket at rectangle
- trim, clip, turn & press
- pin zipper to pocket, aligning with faced slit and sew
- pin pocket onto garment, topstitch

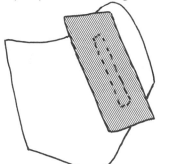 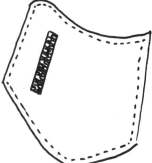

Note: the patch pocket could also be made with a faced slit, as above, instead of the zipper, finish as a buttonhole pocket with 'lips', (page 74) or apply a welt pocket to the patch (page 63).

PATCH POCKETS cont.

Sheers used in conjunction with pocket ideas can be a great combination. Silk organza is my favorite, it has a matt finish. The polyester organza has a sheen to it (it may be easier to find and is very durable). I use organza fabrics quite a bit ...not only to change an undesirable color but also to subdue colors. In the case of a pocket I can cut shapes to applique, stitch them on (cut edges left unfinished). Then cover the whole pocket with a sheer, topstitch to enchance the design and finish with bias strips or as desired.

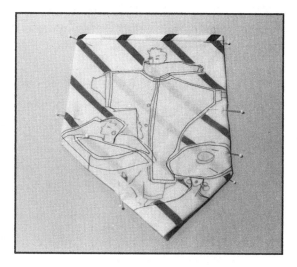

Sometimes I make the whole pocket of the organza. These sheer pockets may be applied to a matching shirt or one made of heavier fabric Enclosed in the two layers of organza are small scraps of most anything you would like to include. Scatter the scraps on the back layer of the pocket and stitch to hold in place. Apply a facing piece cut to match. Stitch, trim, turn & press. This looks very nice if the scraps are 'fancy', sparkley or shiney...so they show up well.

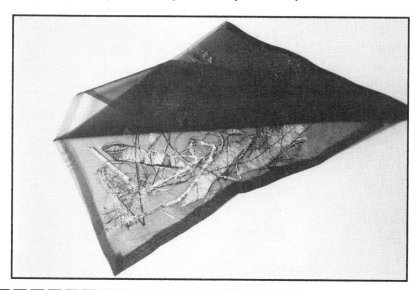

IN-SEAM POCKETS

The pockets in the side seams are very likely the most widely used, as in a pair of pants or in the side seams of a coat or jacket. The pouch section is two pieces, one stitched to the side front and one to the side back where indicated on the pattern. There are many ways to change the original pattern, and make the pocket the most important design element.

The area around the in-seam pocket may be embellished lavishly, with braids or beading or embroidery, with applique or many rows of stitching. These techniques would relate very well to repeating the design on another part of the garment possibly at the cuff area or hem.

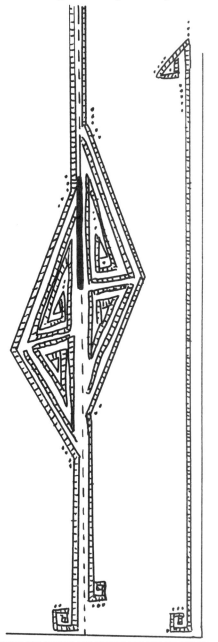

IN-SEAM POCKETS cont.

Having a pocket in a seam that is 1/3 - 1/2 the distance between the side and the center front is a very accessible also logical location. The pocket is put in exactly the same as on the side seams. Here are a some suggestions that would make in-seam pockets very attractive.

On the short jacket use two opposite colors; one for the front panel and the other for the rest of the garment. Stripes would also be terrific, change the directions of the stripes for great graphic appeal.

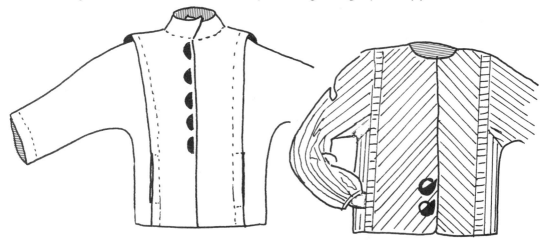

Usually the in-seam pockets are located on each side of the front sections of the coat. Consider extending the front to be an asymetrical opening, then making the pockets in the right hand seam and the other on the very outer edge of the same piece. Great idea!

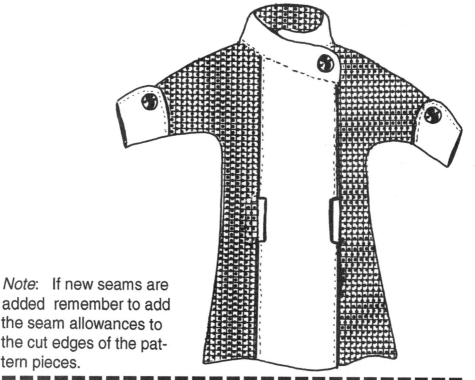

Note: If new seams are added remember to add the seam allowances to the cut edges of the pattern pieces.

IN-SEAM POCKETS, cont.

In addition to patch pockets the technique of facings can be used effectively on vertical pocket applications. Any shape is possible using this versatile technique.

Choose a pattern with an in-seam pocket. The front edge of this in-seam pocket will have some interesting shape. These shapes will be faced to create the top section of the pocket on the front of the garment. These are made to be a part of the seams, usually (but not necessarily) on the side. The facing piece becomes the lining for the shape. The pocket opening could fasten with a button & loop, also consider strip piecing or a stitched design for the insert.

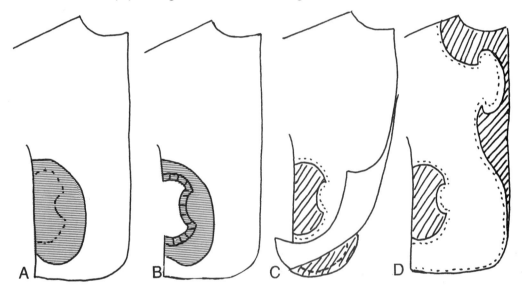

A   B   C   D

METHOD:

* interface front garment section 2" larger than the size of the opening
* cut out 2 pocket pieces, one to be the lining/facing piece-- the other pocket piece, cut from the garment fabric, will be attached to the back of the garment as the in-seam pocket pattern indicates
* stitch lining piece to the outside of garment front, in the shape as designed (A)
* trim, clip, turn & press (B)
* this shape is now the front edge of the pocket (C), the back section will attach to the back side seam and together these two pieces will be the shaped pocket (D)

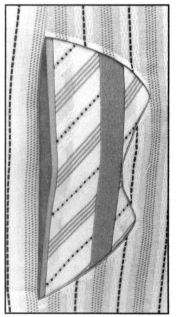

IN -SEAM POCKETS, cont.

Below are just a few ideas to help you create some great but easy pockets for the sides seams of your jackets and coats. When there are numerous faced slits, any or all of them could be pockets, as the first example shows. The second one utilizes quilting as the background medium, this makes a firm pocket. The triangle pointing in, combined with many rows of stitching ending on the button of similar shape all adds up to a nicely defined waist (if you have one). The photograph shows a repeated shape with the pockets and the front opening, the same shapes are echoed on the back of the garment.

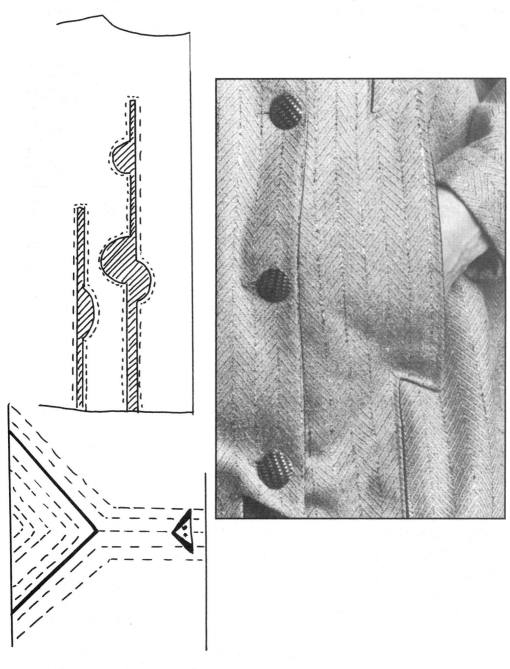

FACED SHAPES

You may need to make a paper pattern to help you decide just what shape and size the pocket is going to be. Oval is the shape that will be shown, but here again -- any shape is possible. Consider relating the shape to some other part of the garment.

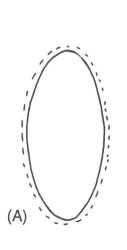
(A)

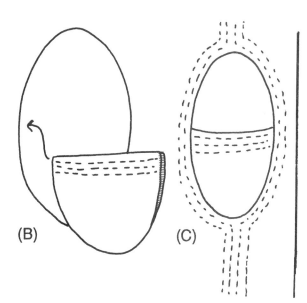
(B)   (C)

METHOD:

- interface the general area where the 'hole' will be placed
- cut a facing of the same fabric or a constrasting one
- pin in place and stitch
- trim, clip, turn & press (A)
- cut 2 oval pieces of garment fabric that are 2" larger than the entire 'hole' around the finished edges (B)
- to make lower portion, fold one piece of oval in half (B)
- place the folded piece on top of the other oval pieces and baste the two pocket pieces together
- align the pocket pieces behind the faced 'hole'
- pin and stitch all layers together, several rows of stitching would be attractive. (C)

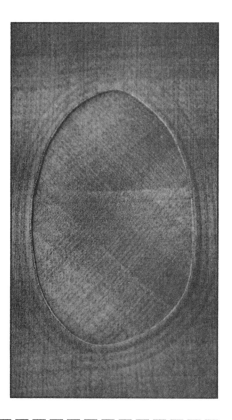

POCKET FLAPS

The size, shape and placement of pocket flaps are up for discussion. Patch pockets very often have flaps. Besides the added interest they also are utilitarian (keeps your 'stuff' from falling out). Usually these flaps are rectangles. I'd like to offer a few suggestions for the shapes. The size is also arbitrary, it can be the same size as the pocket. It could be large, extending beyond the edges of the pocket, possibly to be included a crossing seam (neckline or sleeve area, for instance). The placement is the designer's choice.

Flaps are usually a faced shape (see Techniques). They may be rounded, triangular, freeform. They can be elongated to be included in the shoulder seam, possibly in a contrasting fabric or sewn with piping. If the pocket is plain, the flap can be unique, i.e. an irregular triangle or other asymetrical shape. These finished shapes can be sewn in place above the pocket or included in a seam, i.e. yoke area.

As with most ideas in this book, this is just a place to start... a suggestion for thinking about your project in a slightly different way. It doesn't have to be some incredibly magnificent undertaking... it can simply be a detail like a lowly flap.

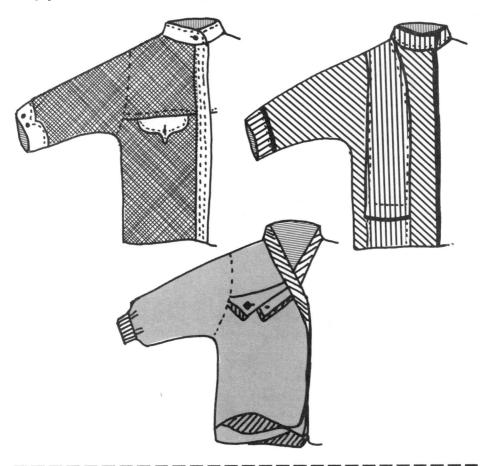

FACED POCKET

When making a pocket opening interface the area of placement. Consider if this will just be a hole or it is to have 'lips' placed behind the faced hole. If the facing need be inconspicuous, use polyester organza, matching the fashion fabric. Draw the shape desired on the facing side and stitch. Clip, trim, turn & press. To make the 'lips' cut two pieces of fabric to match or contrast to the fashion fabric. These pieces need to be at least 1" larger that the size of the hole and interfaced with iron-on interfacing. Place the two pieces, right sides together and baste, as shown. Press back both sides, so stitching is in the middle. These are the 'lips' and are placed in back of the faced hole. To attach them, lift up the fashion fabric layer and pin the facing layer and the 'lips' together. Sew. Topstitching thru all layers is another option that works well. Remove basting on the 'lips'.

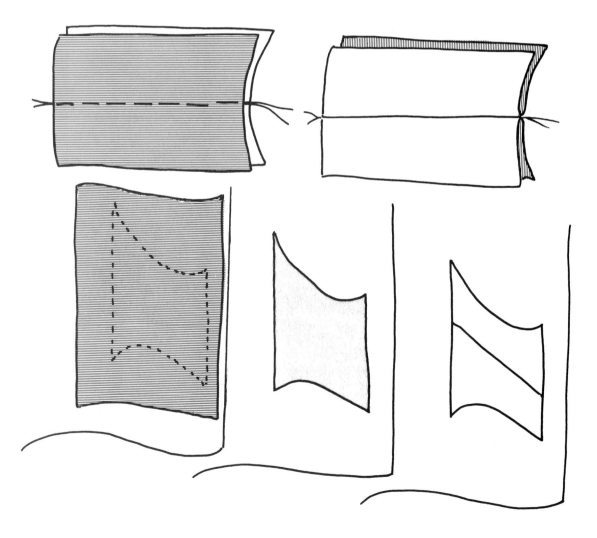

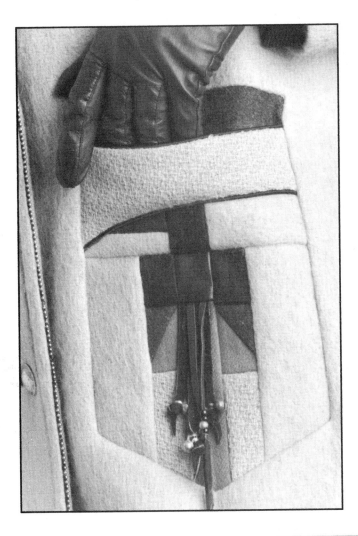

This brushed wool coat has silver 'bead' piping and leather trim. Commercial patterns for the shawl collar jacket and saddle shoulder jacket were overlaid. The length was extended and the lower edge gathered onto a quilted band. The pockets are pieced and inset, then trimmed with metal beads. Hand-crafted buffalo nickel buttons slip very nicely into the bound button-holes. Beautiful jacket by Linda.

Closures

Closures

BUTTONHOLES
TIES AND TABS
BELTS & BUCKLES
BUTTONS
BRACELETS

Unusual closures are my trademark. The closure is an integral part of the design of the garment. It's the last thing to apply when finishing but it needs to be considered at the beginning of the project. I look to find that perfect combination of fabric, color, texture, design and embellishments. Possibly the closure is the prime example of the importance of the relationship concept that was discussed in the first chapter. The shape, texture and overall 'feeling' is so important and can make the garment a special one. An inventive well-chosen closure is for me the pièce de résistance.

The button or other object can inspire the design or the texture of the garment. The outer shape of that object can be repeated by stitching lines, faced shapes or possibly by stencilling. If the object is a heavy one it would be best suited for a quilted wearable.

It's great to have a large collection of treasures from which to choose. I have a cabinet full of pieces purchased from antique or second-hand stores or gifts from friends. I have also found interesting items in stores that sell hardware, boating supplies, sporting goods, electrical equipment. Look beyond what an object is called to the potential for how it could be used for fastening.

Note: Some of the ideas and comments in this chapter were originally published in THREADS, April/May 1989.

BRACELETS

Bracelets make great fasteners and are easy to find in various sizes and materials....wood, bone, metal. Linked bracelets can be divided, the clasp to be used as the fastener. To accentuate a pocket, cuff, or other design feature, consider sewing on the rest of the pieces as well. The one-piece bracelets can easily be used as closures combined with ties or belts.

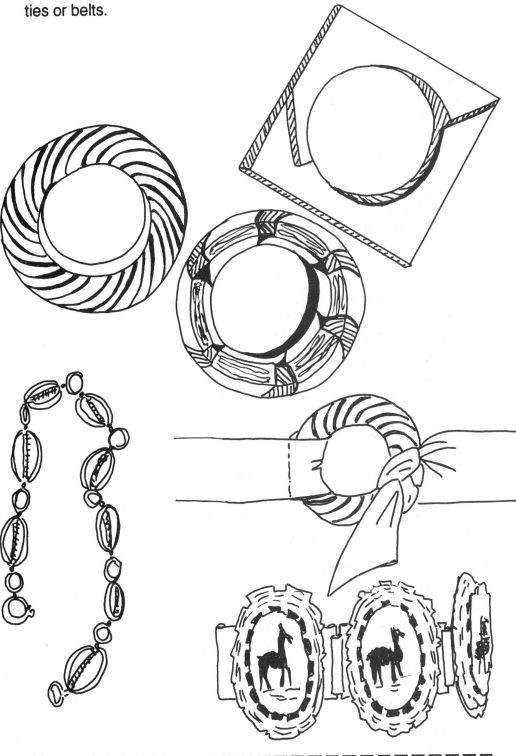

CORDING

Cording is versatile; it can be used for buttonloops, buttonholes, frogs, or trims. It can be purchased, although I rarely find the right size or color so I make it to suit the project.

To make the cording, cut bias strips four times the width of the cord. Measure from the end of cord, the amount of bias to cover, then start with the second measure of cord. The bias will be stitched and turned to cover this first measure of cord. Fold the right side of the fabric over the cord. Using a zipper foot, stitch across the end and down the long side of the bias. When the fabric is a little heavy or hard to turn, it is helpful to stitch a rounded shape at the end of the short side as you turn the corner to the long side. Trim, being careful not to cut the cording. Slide fabric on cording and turn to the right side.

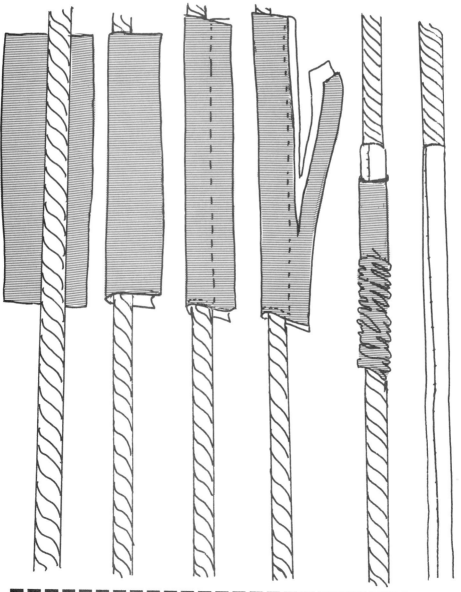

CORDING cont.

When a button is unusually large and has irregular shape, any buttonhole that would accomodate it, just doesn't work. To solve the problem, I attach a covered cording to the opposite side of the garment and wrap the cord around the button to fasten.

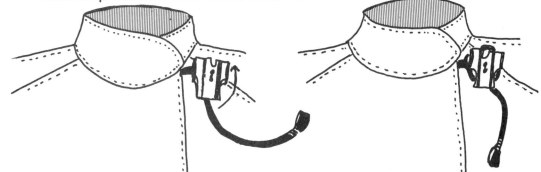

This is the perfect example of noticing how things work. Remember the manila envelopes with the string to wrap around the two buttons? I thought this was an idea worth translating to a garment closure.

Linda's jacket, pictured below, has a corded buttonloop attached with a tab of fabric. The button is sewn a distance away to form a pleat when the sleeve is fastened.

CORDED BUTTONHOLES

Buttonholes can be placed on the edge of a garment by using covered cording. Spaces are left for the buttons. The slits are so subtle that when the garment isn't buttoned they are barely visible and the cording seems to be the trim at the very edge. First sew the buttons to the garment. Then mark, at the right front edge, the top and bottom of the buttons. Cover the cording, or use commercial cording, and handsew to the finished edge on the right side, leaving the slits slightly larger than the buttons. Fasten each end of the 'buttonhole' securely as the cording is stitched on. If there are corners to turn, at the neck edge or elsewhere, tying a simple overhand knot in the cording works well. Consider adding more knots to relate the technique. The cording can start and stop whenever you wish, or when you are at the end of the cording, whichever comes first.

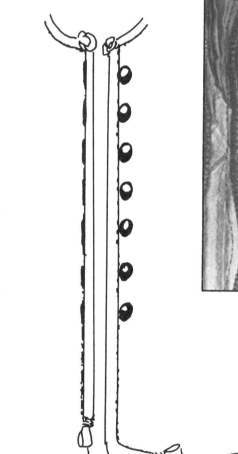

CORDED BUTTONHOLES, cont.

This coat of soft beige wool, with pencil thin cream colored lines, has very full sleeves that button to make a 'cuff'. The collar has one section that is gathered to relate to the sleeves. Cream wool piping and cording accent and finish the coat. The 'striped' mother-of-pearl buttons were a perfect match.

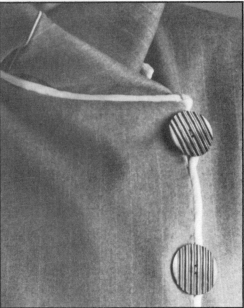

WRAPPING

When covered cording is used for buttonholes, etc., the unfinished ends need some attention. Wrapping the ends is one way to add a finishing detail that works well.

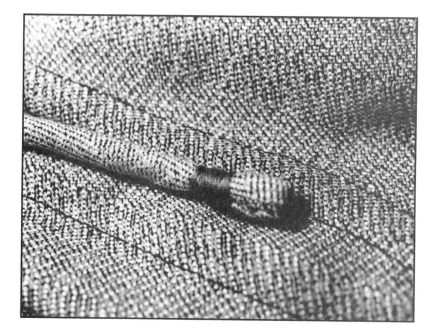

Pull the cording out of the bias tube about 1" or so and cut off cord.

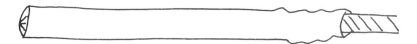

Smooth out the bias and fold under the bias at the 'empty' end 3/4".

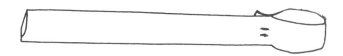

Thread needle. Knot doubled end. Fasten looped end. With the thread still attached to the needle, wrap the doubled thread tightly to cover the unfinished end of the bias tube. Return needle under wrapping. Pull tightly to fasten.

IN-SEAM OR SLOT BUTTONHOLES

This is a method of introducing buttoholes into vertical or horizontal seams by simply leaving slot openings for them. This attractive detail can be added to almost any garment. The buttonholes are placed in a seam by leaving space in the stitching line that connects the seams. These are usually in the seam joining a band to the front edge. This technique can easily be used on garments that do not include this detail, by cutting the pattern and creating a band at the front edge. Add the seam allowances to the cut edges.

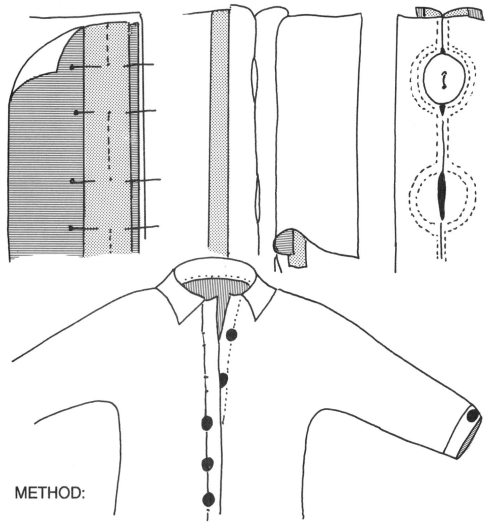

METHOD:

- cut iron-on interfacing 1/2" wide and the length of the band
- apply the strip of iron-on to seam lines on both pieces
- mark the buttonhole placement and stitch as shown, leaving the spaces that are the sizes of the chosen buttons
  Note: reinforce both ends by reverse machine stitching
- fold back the band, and press the seam open
- to finish , topstitch if desired
- the raw edges can be serged or covered by lining

FACED BUTTONHOLES

The technique of faced shapes is perfect for this type of closure. Any shape is possible, either on the very edge or wherever you need a buttonhole. I would like to share my best idea for a closure. The vertical format is the one we'll discuss first. When the facing is applied, the shapes are stitched in as part of the outer edge design rather than a straight edge. The front of the garment needs a firm interfacing. On the facing, draw the design of the shapes at the edge. Stitch, trim, clip, turn & press. To complete the buttonhole, make a piece of covered cording and apply to the outside of the garment or to the facing side. Position the cord so it completes the buttonhole and accomodates the buttons. Hand stitch in place. Finish the end of the cording by wrapping.

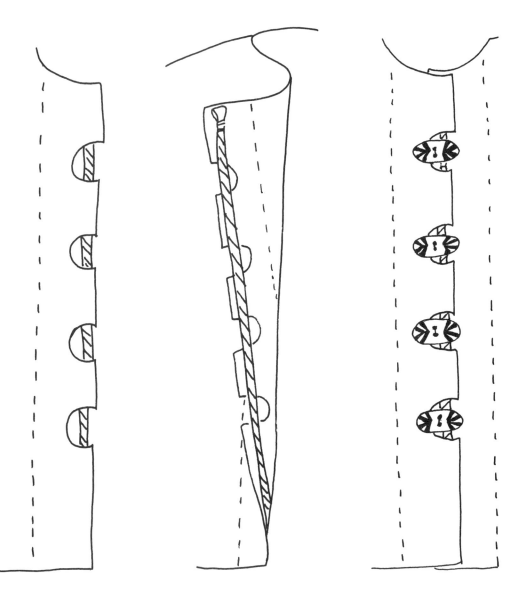

FACED SHAPES, cont.

Cording is sewn behind faced shapes to create 'buttonholes'. Those spaces accomodate large buttons or ones that have irregular shapes.

FACED BUTTONHOLES, cont.

The other similar idea is to incorporate the faced hole with the covered cording. Any shape that you can draw could be a button HOLE (1). Interface the area of the buttonhole. Place facing onto garment where the buttonhole will be, draw the design on the facing if you wish. Make some covered cording, and place the ends into the seam of the hole, at some point. Stitch the hole, cut out the center, clip corners, trim, turn & press. When the facing is turned to the wrong side, the cord will be in view in the center of the hole. Finish the ends of the cording by wrapping and tack to the front of the garment. The two cords that are suspended in the hole are the 'real' buttonhole(2). *Note*: I use polyester organza for the facing, strong and less bulky.

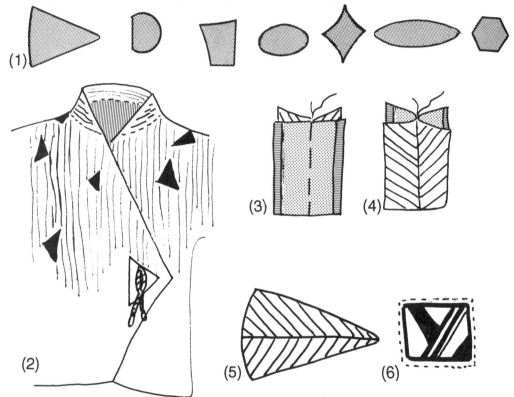

(1) (2) (3) (4) (5) (6)

To make a faced buttonhole that looks like a bound buttonhole, just eliminate the cording step above and add 'lips' to the shaped opening. Cut two pieces of bias twice as wide as the opening to be filled (plus seam allowances) and 1" longer than the opening. Use iron-on Interfacing on the bias pieces, place right sides together. Baste in center (3). Fold back each side and press, this makes the 'lips' (4). Place the 'lips' behind the faced hole (5). Stitch the 'lips' to the shaped hole by lifting the outer layer of fabric and stitching the trimmed seam edges to the edges of the 'lips'. Or topstitch thru all layers (6). Finish the facing with the same method, make a faced hole to line up with the buttonhole, covering the raw edges of 'lips'. Remove basting.

FACED BUTTONHOLES,cont.

Here is another variation on this theme. This gives the opening the look of a buttonhole that has the 'lips' placed in back, without that extra step of applying them.

Cut a facing several inches larger than the opening desired. This may be an oval or a rectangular shaped piece. Sew the facing to the garment, right sides together. Stitch in an eye shape, as shown. Trim, clip to the corners and on the curves. Turn thru the hole, then pull on each end of the facing to arrange properly. The facing fills in the hole, because of the eye-shaped stitching. Since the facing is large, it will be easy to line up the corresponding buttonhole facing on the garment facing side.

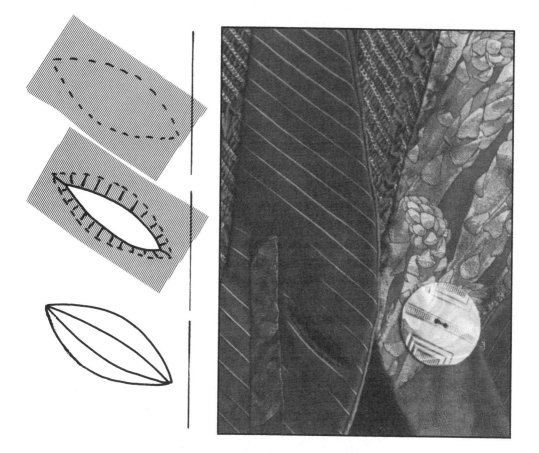

I have also used Ultrasuede and leather for the buttonhole facing on garments that need no structural facings. After clipping, trimming and turning the buttonhole facing, I stitch thru all layers to keep in place. This stitching can be a decorative feature. The square or oval shape of the facing is left, as is, with no companion facing on the wrong side of the garment.

TIES OR TABS

Consider the parts of the garment where a tie is used as the closure... maybe a tie would be the fastener. A tie could fasten a neckline, close a pocket, replace a collar or cuffs. It is a simple solution for many parts of the project that can be effective. The ties need a beginning, somewhere and/or something to fasten to, in addition to the usual solutions. The beginning can always be included in a seam; this solves the unfinished end problem. The unfinished end could also be knotted, covered with an object or pieces of leather. (see page 43 in Sleeves)

To make the ties, decide on the width of the proposed tie then double that and add the seam allowance. Consider the scale and style of the planned garment, so the ties will be in keeping with the wearable: wide for a bulky, casual garment or narrow for a light to medium weight, dressy one. Choices, always choices make. The length is easy; is the tie going to knot or tie in a bow? Will it fasten to a buckle, a toggle or into the open spaces in the button design. Decide on the length, cut the ties, fold in half lengthwise and stitch one end and the length. Trim, turn & press.

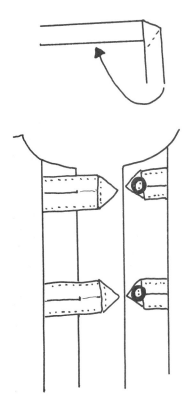
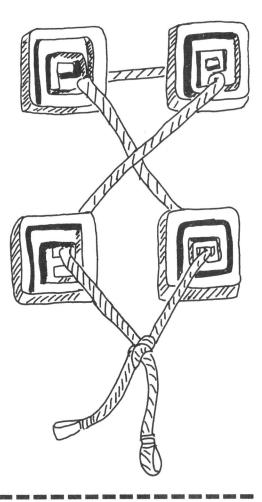

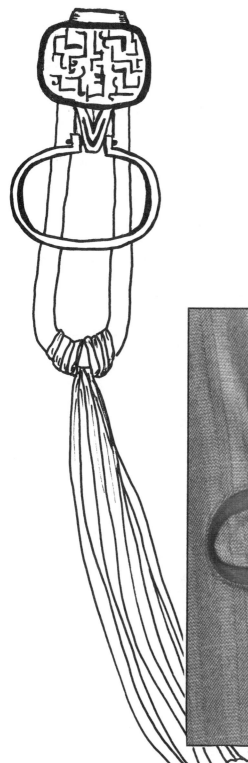

Originally this brass piece was part of a Japanese military uniform. I saw that this shape had definite closure possibilities.

It is important to see beyond the object's original function; to incorporate it into a planned design.

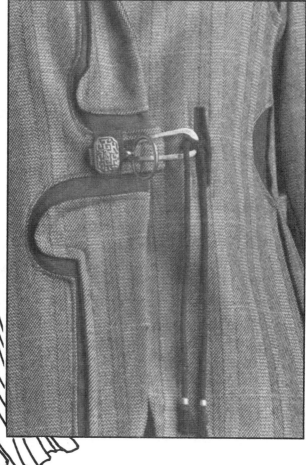

BELTS & BUCKLES

A belt is usually thought of as a long strip of fabric with a buckle at the end. The difference between a tie and a belt is usually the length.

Buckles are something that I have collected for many years, along with buttons. It seems natural to ask for both when I enter the antique store. The belts, of course, are the perfect union for the buckles. If the belt is to be softly folded into the buckle it could be wider than the opening in that buckle. If it is to be flat, then it would have to be the same or slightly narrower than the opening. What keeps the belt in place? Carriers or belt loops are the least obtrusive, followed by buttons to keep the belt in place. The hem of the garment could also serve as the carrier. Make buttonhole where the belt is to surface and attach a gorgeous buckle to the end.

Thread carriers are easy to make and hardly noticeable. To make one, bring up long doubled thread, or pearl cotton, thru the fabric. Take a small stitch at the designated mark for the other end of the carrier. Return needle to beginning point and take another small stitch. Sew buttonhole stitches over the loose threads, pulling thread tightly to create a firm carrier.

1. under threads
   leave loop

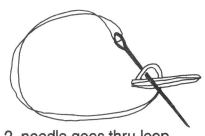

2. needle goes thru loop
   pull tightly

BELTS & BUCKLES cont.

Trench coats have always been popular and probably will continue to be so. The back of the coat has an outsized loose panel that looks like a long yoke. If the panel were extended to the waist area, the belt could be buttoned to it.

The belt could be sewn in a seam ... on the sides of a garment or in the front. If there is no front panel on the pattern you wish to work with, cut the pattern and add the seam allowance. Consider using an entirely different fabric in the front section, maybe a ribbed knit. The belt that is inserted in that seam will show up nicely against this contrasting fabric.

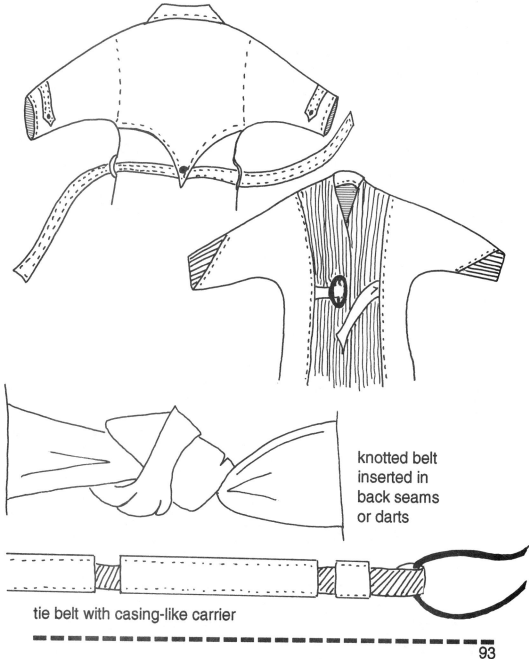

knotted belt inserted in back seams or darts

tie belt with casing-like carrier

PLACEMENT

There are times when the closure needs to be rather tailored and staightforward. Maybe the buttons and buttonholes could be arranged in a more unusual way. The new machines make wonderful buttonholes so easily, this may be an idea to think about for a future project. Make many, many buttonholes... you don't need to cut them all, because just a few will be used. (1)

If the reverse were true and there were a lot of buttons, sew buttons to the right of the buttonholes, as well as on the left side of the garment.(2)

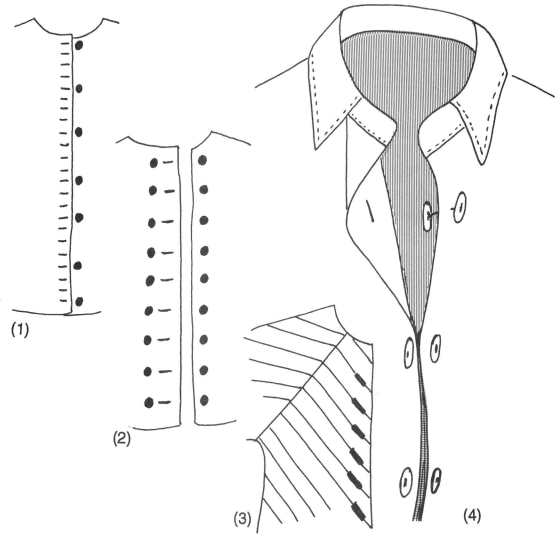

(1)

(2)

(3)

(4)

When cutting stripes or plaids on a bias front, place the buttonholes on the diagonal. This actually makes the buttonholes on the straight grain. (3)

On a jacket or coat that has two or three buttons to fasten, why not sew extra buttons underneath each one on the facing side, so it could be buttoned by overlapping (the normal way) or like a French cuff. When it is buttoned the two front edges will be brought to the outside.(4)

BUTTONS

Most sew-ers have button collections, so that would be a good place to start looking for that special closure. If the buttons are flat ones with holes thru them, notice if the back side has a better color or texture than the front. If so, use the 'wrong' side up. Consider combining nonmatching buttons that have the same color, similar design or size. Maybe the shape of the button is great but the color isn't to your liking, paint it with acryllics. To easily add a little pizazz it may be a matter of positioning the buttons, by uneven spacing. If the buttons I have chosen are ordinary, I use them in an unexpected way.

If the buttons have very large holes, consider using a cord to hold them in place. This would replace sewing them on with thread, that would be out of scale with the size of the button. If there are only one or two buttons, I use one piece of cording for each. Tack the center of a 6" piece of cording (or braid) to the garment, slide the cording thru the holes in the button, tie a square knot to secure.

If there are many buttons to attach, I slide all on a flat braid or cord and position them where desired. Then the braid or cord is sewn by hand to the garment, each button is not individually applied.

Gallery

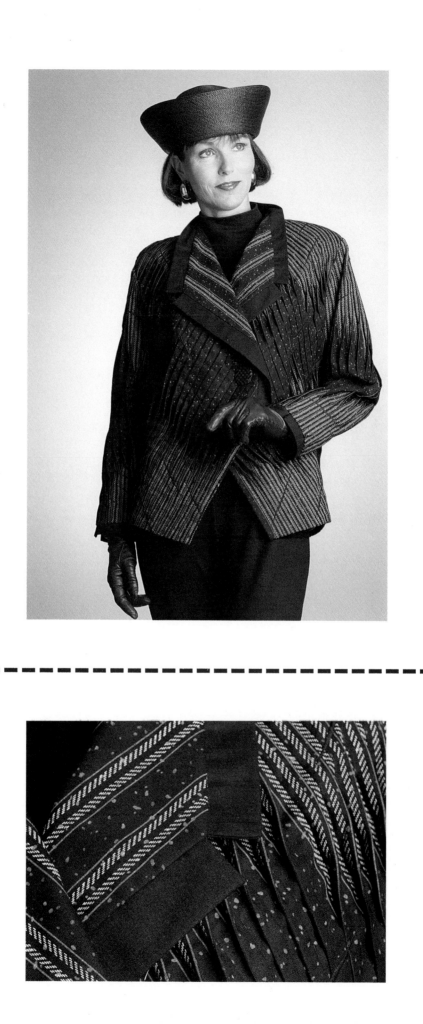

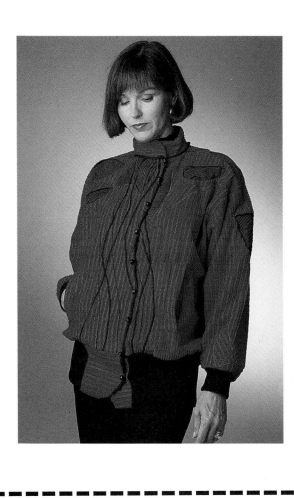

112

Gallery

Hems

Hems

FLAT
CORDED
PIPED
IRREGULAR
UNEVEN
FLOUNCED
FLARED
TAPERED
STIFFENED
TOPSTITCHED
PADDED
QUILTED
RIBBED
LAYERED

The dictionary defines the hem as an edge made by folding back a margin of cloth and sewing it down. RIGHT! That is certainly one way of looking at it. There are many creative solutions so let's get to the bottom of it all!

NARROW HEM

A narrow hem is probably the easiest of all, because it requires virtually no easing, since there is little difference between the raw edge and the fold.

METHOD:

- turn up the hem along hemline & press
- trim the hem allowance to 5/8"
- turn under the raw edge, to meet the crease & press
- turn up on hemline and stitch, consider two rows of stitching
  Note: if your sewing machine has a narrow hemmer attachment, the hem can be done in one step. Trim hem to 1" then hem.

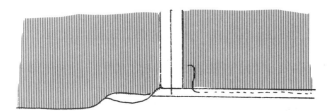

TOPSTITCHED HEM

If topstitching is a part of the design of a garment, a stitched hem would be a consideration. To keep a balanced look, the stitching rows will then be the same distance from the edge as the other stitching. This hem works easily on a fairly straight garment.

METHOD:

- fold up hem 1' - 1 1/2" & press
- serge raw edges or turn under & press
- pin hem in place, matching seams allowances of garment
- topstitch, as many rows as desired

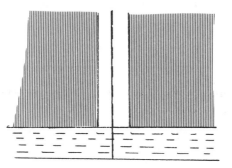

TAPERED HEMS

I find that when there is a problem to solve, I can zero in on it with gusto. Sometimes I create a problem just to figure out how many solutions and possibilities I can think of...new ideas and answers don't materialize if I keep doing things the same old way.

What are the various techniques to narrow the hem area of a garment? Tapering the lower edge of a garment, is worth some thought. One *probable* answer is to gather or pleat the excess fabric onto a band of fabric. Another idea is to use ribbing.....I don't just mean a little 3" band of ribbing -- I mean RIBBING! 12" wide (finished, so that measurement would be doubled). It would be predictable cutting the ribbing 6'-8' then folding that in half, so why do what is expected? Consider applying the ribbing just on the back of the jacket. When the doubled ribbing is applied to finish the hem of a jacket or coat, stretch it slightly as it is sewn to the garment. Serge all the cut edges to finish. To relate the ribbing at the hemline to the other detailing on the garment, I apply it to the cuffs, collar or just the top to a patch pocket.

Tucks and tunnels are another possibility for tapering. These tucks will be very attractive when 6"-8" in length. The tuck could be sewn so the fold of fabric is on the inside or the outside, as a decorative detail. The location of these tucks or tunnels might be on both sides of the garment, from side back to side front. Or you might choose the center back, then repeat on the front.

PADDED HEMS

A finish that reminds me of Japanese clothing is a padded hem. Some of the more elegant kimonos had very large piping in the hem. This rounded finish would be appropriate when the hem is to be quite firm and accentuated, very likely the only eyecatching detail on the jacket or coat. The cording applied with cut bias strips, might be 1 1/2"-2". If your local fabric store doesn't carry this large size cording, inquire at an upholstery shop. When using a cording this large, it is especially important to taper the ends at the points connecting it with other seams.

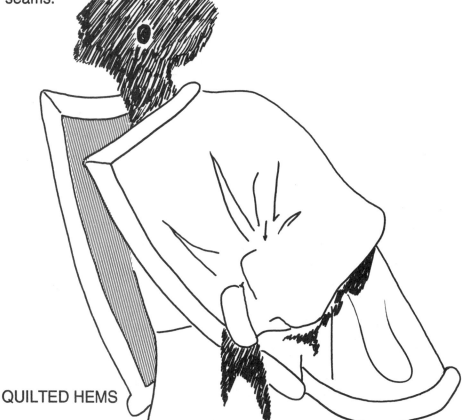

QUILTED HEMS

Applying a wide quilted band to the lower edge of a garment gives it a wonderful 'weighted' hem. Consider, when planning this finish, where the band lines up on the body. This technique has the tendency to accentuate the horizontal. Maybe a contrasting fabric with this added padding, wouldn't be great on the hips but on the hem of a long coat it could be sensational. Of course, it can also be made of matching fabric, applied with just a narrow piping of a contrasting color.

Method: Stitch right side of band to wrong side of garment at the hemline. Press this seam. Choose a very thin batting, cut it 1/2" narrower than the band. Place batting on top of the garment, lining it up with the lower seam. Fold the band over the batting turning in about 1/2" at the top. Pin profusely (or baste) all layers together. Stitch in rows or other design as desired.

OUTSIDE HEMS

If the fabric of the garment is double-faced, the same on both sides or not the same (and it doesn't matter) then consider turning the hem to the outside. This opens up some interesting ideas. I would cut the garment so the hem is at least 6" wide....let's make a 'statement' here.

The top of the hem might have a casing at the edge to accomodate a covered cording or other ties/belts. Flat felled seams, on the side seams of the garment, make a good finish for right or wrong surface. After the front facing is sewn on, and the jacket is ready for the hem, there is one last decision. The right front will lap over the left so the left tie cannot end at the front edge. A buttonhole, sewn on the front part of the casing in the appropriate place, is an easy solution. The tie will be threaded thru until it comes to the buttonhole then it 'surfaces' and will tie to the other side.

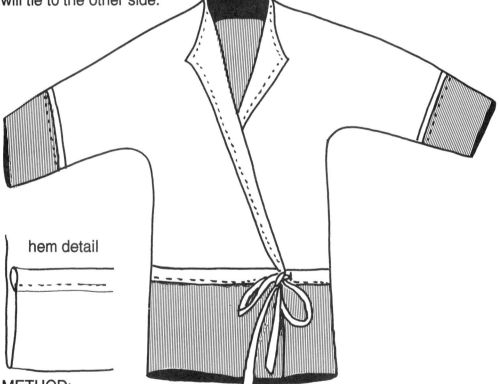

hem detail

METHOD:
- cut bias casing 1"wider than the cording
- stitch one side of bias to top edge' wrong' side of hem, *Note:* as hem folds up, the 'right' side of garment is the 'wrong' side of the hem
- mark buttonhole placement & make buttonhole thru one thickness only, interfacing buttonhole
- fold bias in half, baste bias to garment thru all thicknesses
- 'stitch in the ditch' just below casing, thread cording thru finish ends of cording with a simple knot
- stitch front edge of hem to front, at faced edge

OUTSIDE HEMS cont.

Looking at a landscape painting gave me a wonderful design idea. A pattern created a background where the lower edge of the trees and bushes juxtaposed to the foreground. To connect all this rhetoric with a sewing project, the procedure on the preceding pages, without the casing, is one interpretation.

The lower edge is cut in a freeform design. This edge is finished with a narrow hem, a bias strip or with a faced shape (see Techniques). All the finishes for this edge are applied to the wrong side, since it eventually becomes the right side.

Suggestions for the section above the hemline of the garment: piecing, applique or possibly a print. As the lower section is turned up to cover the raw edges of the upper portion, a nice contrast occurs. After the hem is folded up, the lower portion could be stitched in a design or left plain, as desired.

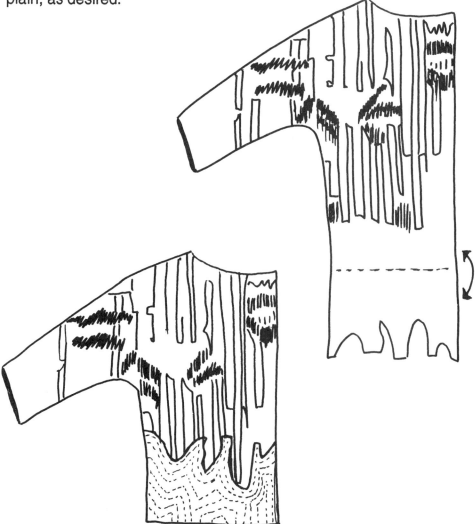

IRREGULAR HEMS

Faced shapes on the bottom of the garment is an easy way to achieve great results. These shapes can begin as part of the front opening and continue on, to the hemline. There may be several shapes placed on top of one another.

Whole panels, as front sections, could be faced and loose from the adjoining pieces. Topstitching would emphasize the lines created and could also serve to sew pieces together, if desired.

Consider facings shaped like triangles, rounds, squares or ? ..... to suit the design. These would simply be cut by adding the shape to the pattern piece plus a facing piece to match. Interfacing will add needed firmness. Always interface the hems, no matter what shape they are, especially on a 'regular' one.

Linings

Linings

Text & drawings in this chapter by Guest Author, Linda Wakefield

Linings are one of the best ways to add quality, wearability and comfort to your coat or jacket. Choose a fabric that will be appropriate for your garment, both in weight and fabric. China silk is great choice for lining a lightweight jacket, but would be too fine for a melton wool coat. Coat weight fabrics are better supported by medium to heavy weight satin, taffeta or milium coat lining. An unusual cotton print might be a great choice for a sporty style 'baseball' jacket, with a sleeve lining of something more slippery (to slide easily over a sweater or blouse).

Be creative, make the lining something to look forward to and a special surprise on the inside. Consider pockets in the lining -- put them wherever you want!

Note: Some of the comments in this chapter may have appeared in THREADS magazine.

LININGS

Garment lined to the edge

Often a pattern will supply no lining pieces. Some styles, a cardigan for example, could be lined to the edge.

• Use the same pattern pieces as the outer garment.
• Cut the outer fabric first, then lay the pattern pieces (outer fabric is attached) onto lining fabric.
  The outer fabric will act as a 'weight' and cutting around it will make the lining slightly larger than the garment, ensuring that it will hang properly and not pull.

• Lining is right sides together
• Place center back line 1 1/2" -2" from fold of fabric for ease pleat.
• Stitch at neckline, as indicated, just above waistline and hem for about 1" to form pleat.
• Press pleat to one side.

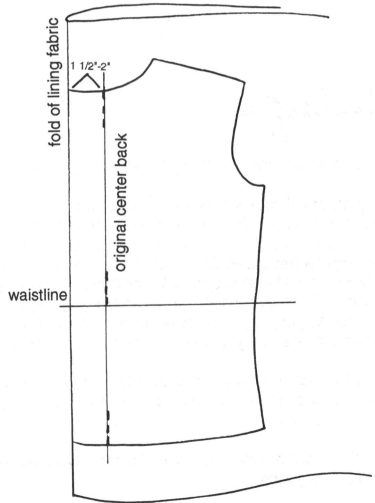

LININGS, cont.

To draft the front lining:

• Trace around the jacket front
• Overlay front facing onto the front

• Transfer stitching line 1/2" inside facing edge, onto traced front

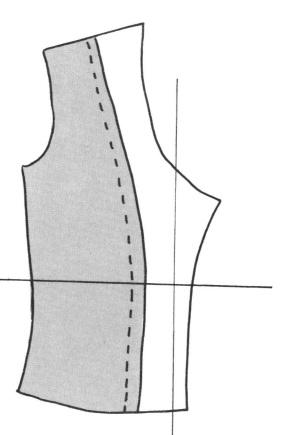

• Add l/2" seam allowance to that stitching line

• The shaded area represents the front lining piece. Use it with the original facing piece of the pattern.

• The back may have a neck or yoke type facing. Prepare the pattern for the lining the same way as the front.

• Cut the lining pieces the same length as the garment. This makes them easier to handle and will ensure sufficient length to hang properly.

• Seam lining and front facing together, leaving a 4" opening along lower side edge of facing to hem lining.

• Construct the lining as if it were a duplicate garment.

• Stitch back pleat, as indicated on page 127.

• Attach front to back at shoulder and side seams.

• Set in sleeves.

• Proceed at neckline and front edge according to pattern instructions. (with lining attached at facing)

• Turn inside out thru lower edge.

• Align shoulder seams of lining and garment, then pin together.

• Align side seams and sleeve seams at armscye.

• Reach up in between the garment and lining. Attach the seam allowances to each other at the back armscye for 1 1/2".

• The garment should hang overnight at this point before it is hemmed.

LININGS, cont.

When hemming the lower edge of a garment and sleeves it is important to support these hems by inserting interfacing.

• Cut a strip, 2" wide of *bias* interfacing (A)
• Attach this slightly below the center of the bias strip at the hemline. This will distribute bulk in the finished hem as if it were 'graded'.
• Steam press hem into position leaving cut edge flat.
• Roll edge back about 3/8" and hem loosely *between* layers. (B)

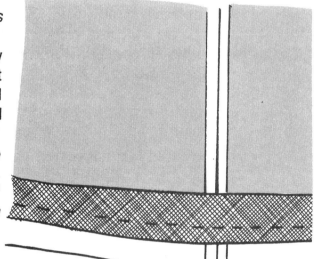

(A)

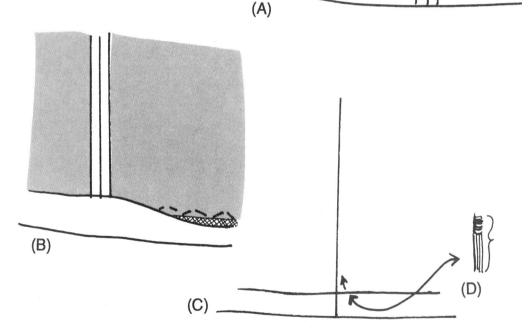

(B)

(C)

(D)

When hemming a coat, the lining will be hemmed separately from the garment.
• Turn up hem so that it falls about 1"-2" shorter than the coat but still cover the coat hem (C)
• Hem lining and press.
• At side seams make a 1" long thread tack, between lining and coat hems, to keep in place. (D))
• Buttonhole stitch over several strands of thread.

LININGS, cont.

Lining hems
Also sleeve lining hems for jackets or coats

• Hem jacket lower edge same as coat.
• To pin lining hem, lay jacket over ironing board, back neck edge extended over round edge of board. This will create a curve in the lining length at the center back to ensure that the jacket won't 'buckle' because the lining is too short.

• Fold up lower lining edge, pressing and forming an ease pleat 3/4" from hem at jacket edge. (A)
• Pin in place about 1" above ease pleat. (B)
• Hang jacket or try on to check that the garment hangs smoothly.

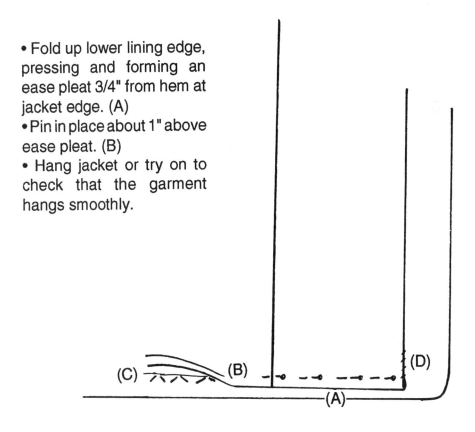

• The ease pleat that is formed should not have to function for the garment to hang properly. It is a 'wearing ease' pleat.

To hem lining, lay folded lining edge away from hem. Hand stitch the hem of lining to hem of jacket, being careful to catch only these 'inside' layers. (C)

• Finish lower side edge of lining by hand after forming the lining hem pleat. (D)

Patterns

Patterns

Text & drawings in this chapter by Guest Author, Linda Wakefield

You are the designer! This allows you the ultimate freedom in creating your garment and presents the challenge of how to convert your design into a realilty. This chapter is a tool to bridge that gap and build your confidence.

Guidelines for combining patterns:
- Choose patterns that are the same size (or size range, combine a 'small' with a size 6 or 8).
- Align common lines/markings (center front lines, waist-lines, center back lines, etc.).
- Pattern manufacturers use standard measurements so patterns from various companies can be easily combined.
- Adding a new collar (or sleeve) will require that the body of the garment be changed to accommodate the new part. The new collar and *both* the old and new body pieces will be needed to construct the pattern.
  The neckline (or armhole) of the new body will need to be altered to match the neckline (or armhole) into which the new collar fits.

Relax, examples follow.

PATTERNS

As a designer, I have a few basic styles of coats and jackets that I like to use. They are a known entity -- both in fit and appeal. I like to continue to use those basic styles and develop them to my current ideas.

For example, a cocoon style jacket is comfortable, roomy and a for-giving' fit for many body types. It can be transformed into a more current "Southwest" style jacket by adding a shawl collar and lacing the collar and hem edges with leather. (see Techniques for leather lacing)

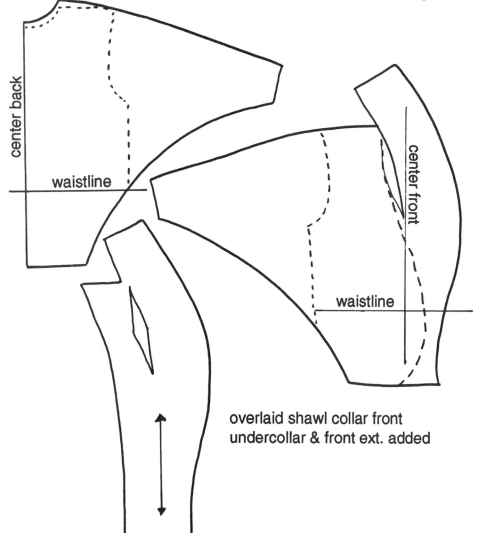

overlaid shawl collar front
undercollar & front ext. added

• The body pieces of the cocoon jacket need to be adjusted to accomo-date the shawl collar.
• Convert the front and back necklines and blend shoulder lines, as necessary.
• With these simple changes, the existing shawl collar (uppercollar and facing) piece can be used as is.

PATTERNS, cont.

Convert a cardigan, from a set-in sleeve, to a raglan sleeve

• The neckline area of the sleeve may need to be trimmed to match
  front and back neckline of cardigan.

•Now the raglan sleeve pattern can be used.

•Since the neckline of the cardigan hasn't been changed, the original
  front and back facings can be used.

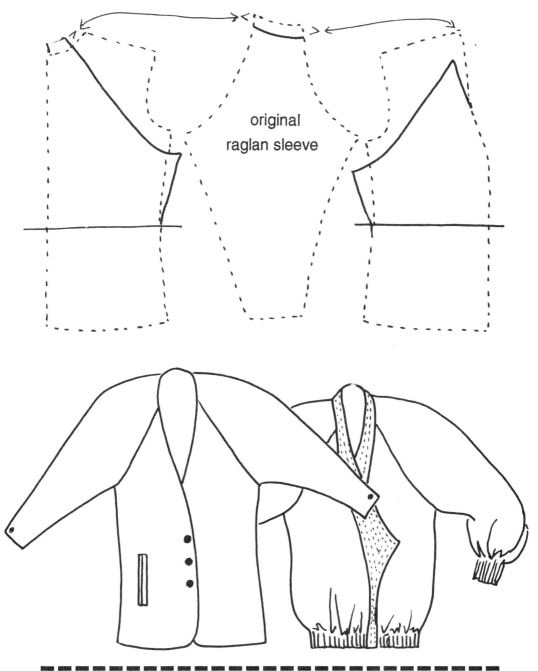

original
raglan sleeve

Convert a cardigan style to a tailored blazer collar with lapels

• Changes: Altered neckline, shoulders and front (A) to fit the upper and under collar, front facing and lapel of the blazer style. (B)

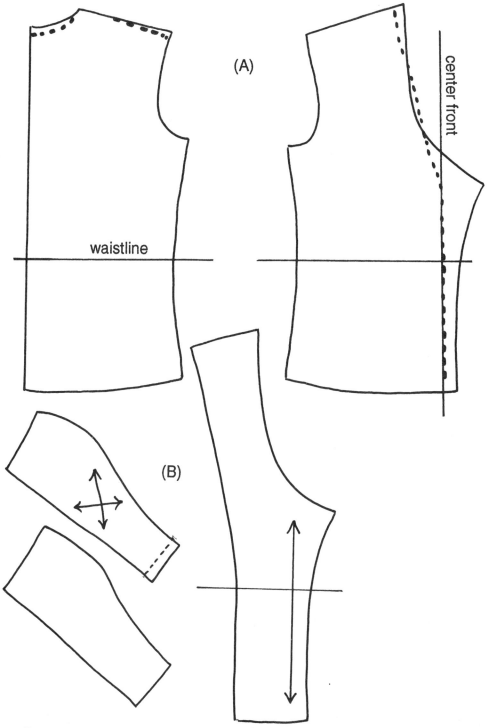

• Original pieces for blazer collar with lapels that will now fit the altered body pattern.

PATTERNS, cont.

Convertible, asymmetrical lapel /closure jacket

An unusual and appealing jacket can be easily adapted from a 'baseball' style jacket pattern or one with a loose fitting plain front. *Note:* If the pattern is fitted thru the midriff, this simple lapel will not roll properly.

• Trace the complete front.

• Redraw left front neckline into a 'v' shape, from the shoulder to the bustline (fig. A). Cut both the left front and lining from this piece.

• Draw neckline curve from right shoulder onto left front, then angle back toward hem. These right front lines are overlapping the left front. (fig. A)

Other shapes could be drawn; consider how this will be positioned relative to the bustline, both open and closed. Plan the point of the lapel several inches above or below the bustline for the most flattering line.

• While the jacket is in the pattern stage, it is recommended that you roll the lapel, as if it were open to check the position. Consider the finished edge relative to the armhole and bustline, adjust if necessary.

• The approximate roll line is indicated. (B) The lapel/facing piece should extend well inside the roll line. The facing is indicated by the shaded area. The remainder is the right front lining. Be sure to add seam allowances to these edges.

• Use this lapel pattern for your interfacing also.

The jacket and lining, with lapel/facing attached are assembled as two separate parts. With right sides together, the jacket right front edge, from hem to the point is seamed together with the corresponding edge of the facing you have created.

Finish the lower edge with ribbing or an elasticized band. The remaining raw edges, from the right front point, around the neckline extending the entire left front edge to the hem is finished with a 2" wide quilted band.

PATTERNS, cont.

Convertible, asymmetrical lapel/closure jacket

- Consider the lapel section for beading, lace or embroidery
- Double line indicates new right front (D)
- Single outline is new left front (E)
- Right front lapel/facing (C)

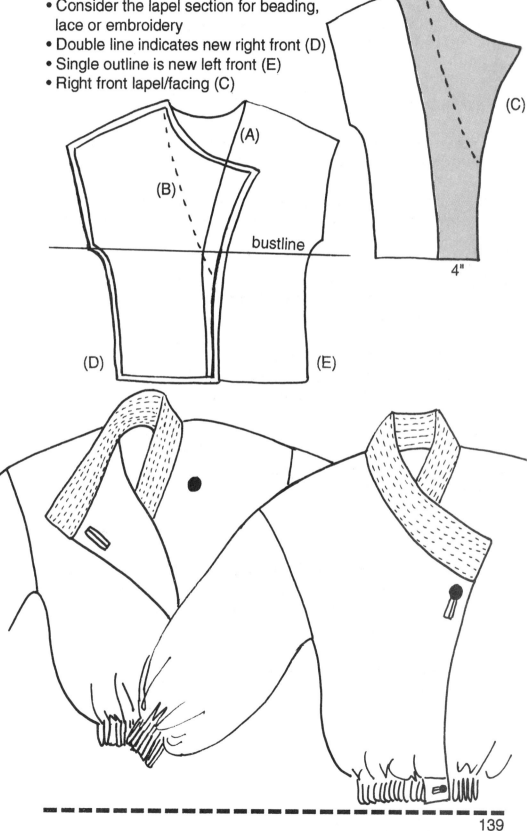

PATTERNS, cont.

Sleeves
• Gathers at both cap and wrist.

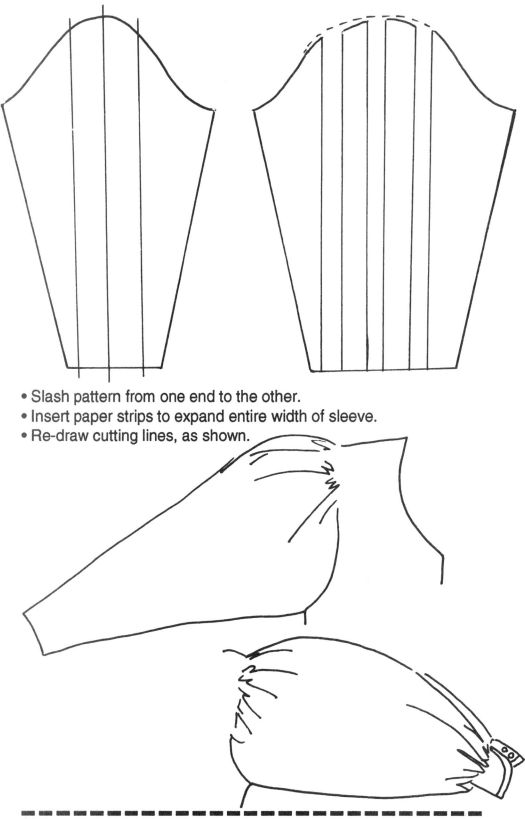

• Slash pattern from one end to the other.
• Insert paper strips to expand entire width of sleeve.
• Re-draw cutting lines, as shown.

PATTERNS, cont.

Sleeves
To add gathers to a sleeve:

• Consider the thickness of the fabric to be used. -- thick fabric will not
  have 'room' to gather up as much as lightweight fabric.
• Make a sample of gathering before expanding the sleeve and cutting.
• Slash sleeve pattern and insert 'wedges'. Re-draw cutting line along
  altered area, as shown.

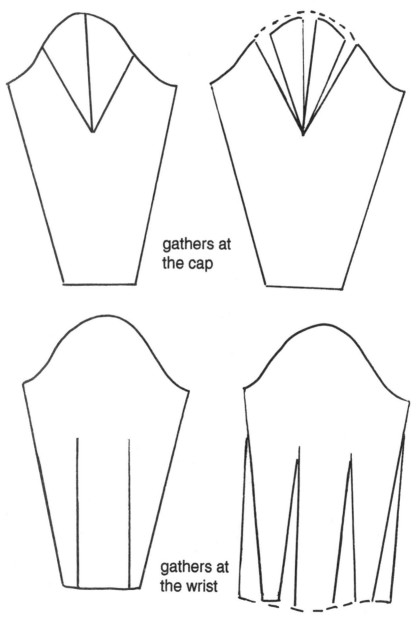

gathers at
the cap

gathers at
the wrist

• As in figure above, slash sleeve and insert 'wedges'.
• Also add 'wedges' to sides.
• Re-draw lower edge, curving as shown.

PATTERNS, cont.

Changes to the existing sleeve:

- Pleats, tucks, smocking and other manipulations
- Often it is easier to prepare the fabric as desired and then cut the sleeve from the original pattern, rather than draft the changes.

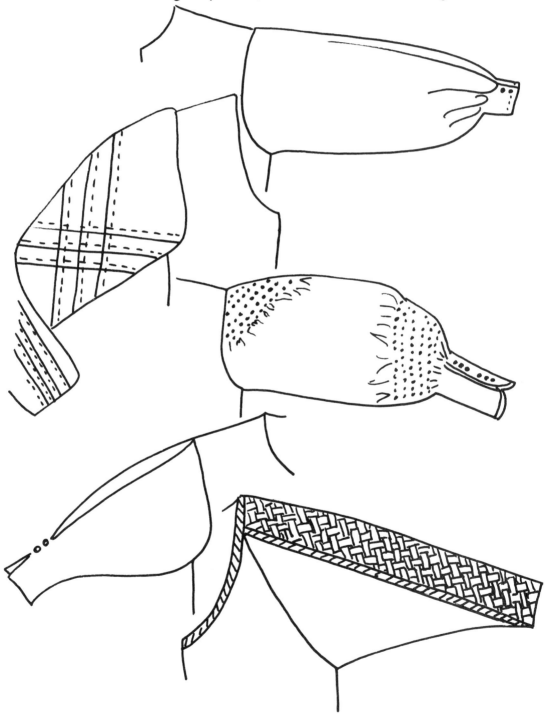

PATTERNS, cont.

Drafting a cuff

To shorten the sleeve for a fitted cuff:
• Remember to allow for the thickness of the fabric around the fore-
  arm.
• Allow sufficient ease for a comfortable fit.
• If the cuff is narrow, finished width about 2", a waistband method of
  application could be used.
• Anything over 2" wide will need to be shaped.

  > For instance, to make a 4" wide cuff measure the wrist and the
  > arm 4" above the wrist. These should be loose measurements.
  > If this is an outergarment, consider the thickness of what will be
  > worn underneath. Measure loosely over those garments.

• Cut a 4" wide paper strip, the wrist measurement plus wearing ease
  (1" to 2" ease for a jacket or coat).

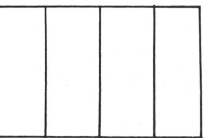

Slash paper at even intervals.

• Overlay slashed paper onto another sheet. Spread slashes, at one
  edge, to fore-arm measurement plus ease.

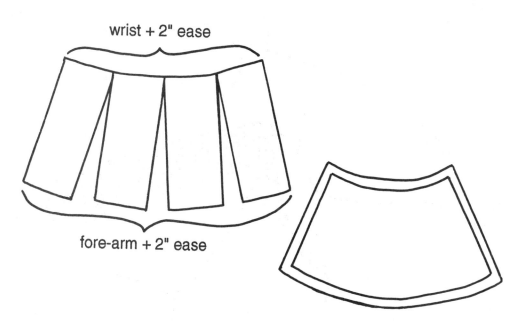

wrist + 2" ease

fore-arm + 2" ease

•Trace adjusted edges to new pattern and add seam allowances to all
  edges.

PATTERNS, cont.

Asymmetrical yoke

• Fold pattern paper in half.
• Trace front pattern piece of garment, or back if preferred.
• Arrange center front line on fold of pattern paper.
• Cut out folded tracing through both layers.
• This will be the completed front with centerline marked by fold.
• Open out and lay this whole front flat.

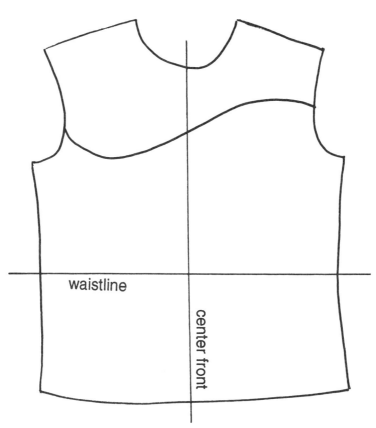

waistline

center front

• Draw desired yoke seam line thru front. Consider the effect and the
  placement of the yoke line on the body. A pleasing proportion of yoke
  size to jacket length might also be a consideration.
• Separate the fronts at the center line for opening.
• Extend lengthwise at center front line for an overlap, if desired, and
  add seam allowance.
• Construct with facing or binding to finish the edges.
**Note: If two distinct right and left fronts have been created, use
caution when cutting pieces 'right' side up on fabric.**
• Separate the pattern at the yoke seam line. This is the stitching line.
• Be sure to add seam allowances to both edges, the lower edge of
  yoke and the matching upper edge of the body.

PATTERNS, cont.

Asymmetrical yoke, other shapes

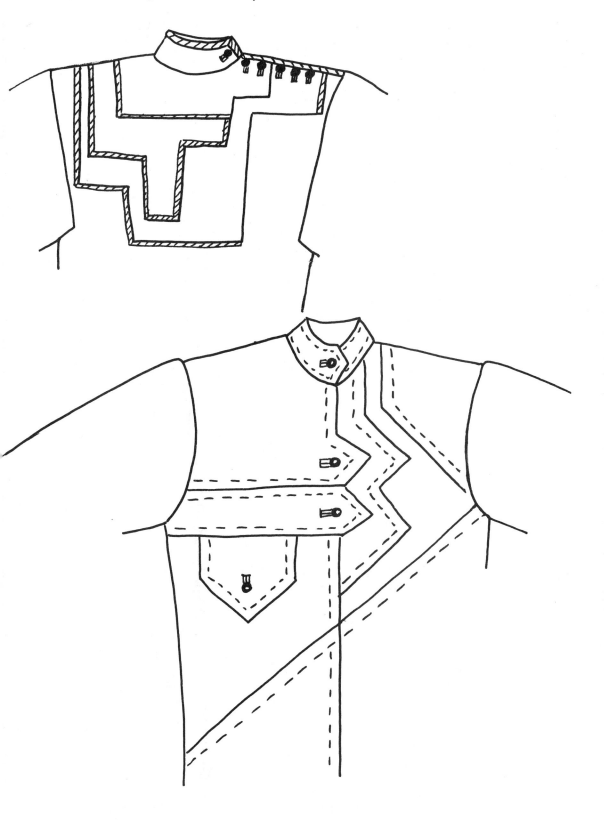

PATTERNS, cont.

Asymmetrical closure & hems

- Fold pattern paper and prepare tracing of garment front, as described on preceding page -- asymmetrical yokes.
- Open out paper and draw desired outlines for 'new' edges.
- *Note*: Dotted line indicates facing line.

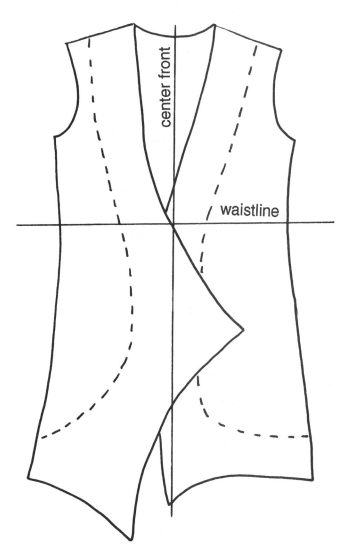

- The example above illustrates a new neckline and right front edge extending to a point near the left side seam. This would be a good place for an interesting fastening. From this point the edge curves and angles again at the hemline.
- Choose a pleasing arrangement, considering how this will appear against your skirt, trousers or legs, as appropriate.
- Trace each of the right and left fronts according to the new outlines.
- Add seam allowances to the new edges.

PATTERNS, cont.

Asymmetrical closures & hems

- To finish the newly created edges, it is best to draft a facing for each.
- Trace the pattern edges, including part of the shoulder and side cutting lines, for their angle.
- Draw in facing edge, as indicated by dotted lines on drawing opposite.
- A reverse facing, finished on the outside, is another way to handle this edge.
- Perhaps the edge, toward the body, will echo the angles of the finished edge.
- The facing edge could be piped or bound then stitched in place.

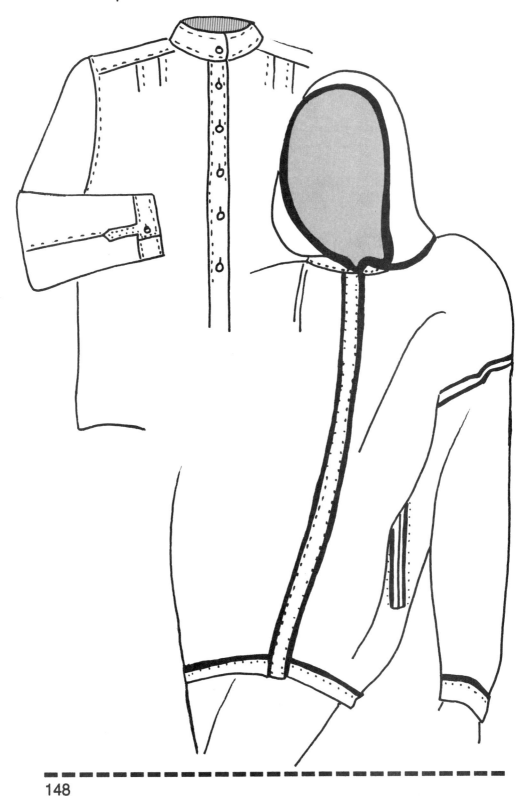

PATTERNS, cont.

The hood pattern on the opposite page can be added to any round neckline. The drawing below is one example of a style that would accomodate a hood. Hoods are great additions to sweatshirts, jackets, coats or capes. Hoods can be detachable.

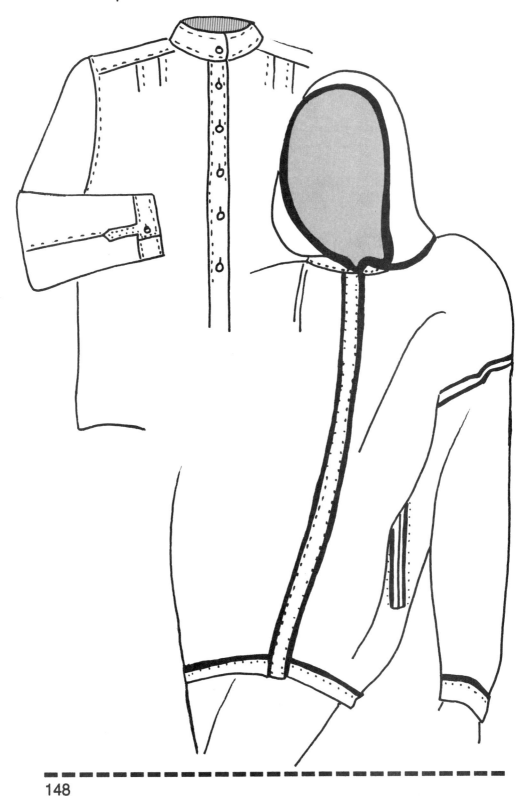

PATTERNS, cont.

Hood Pattern

This hood is intended for a round neckline. Gather the lower edge to fit the neckline. The front edge is bound, or the hood can be lined. Included in the dimensions are 1/2" seams. Each square = 1".

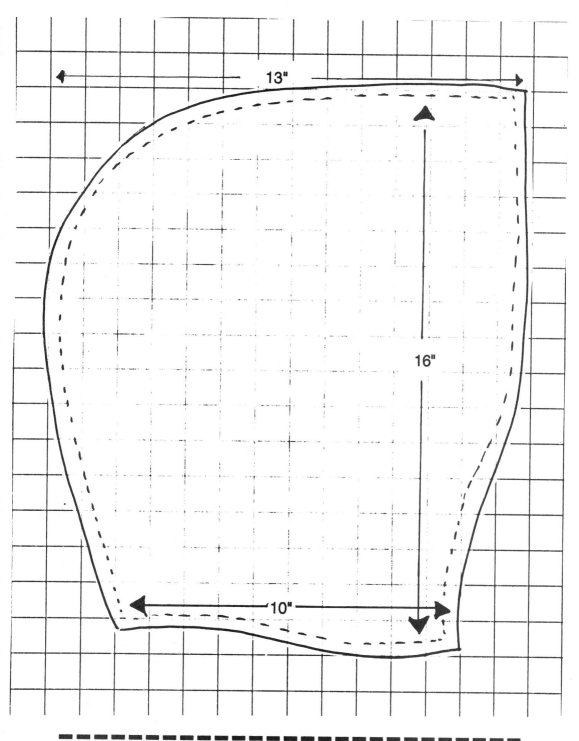

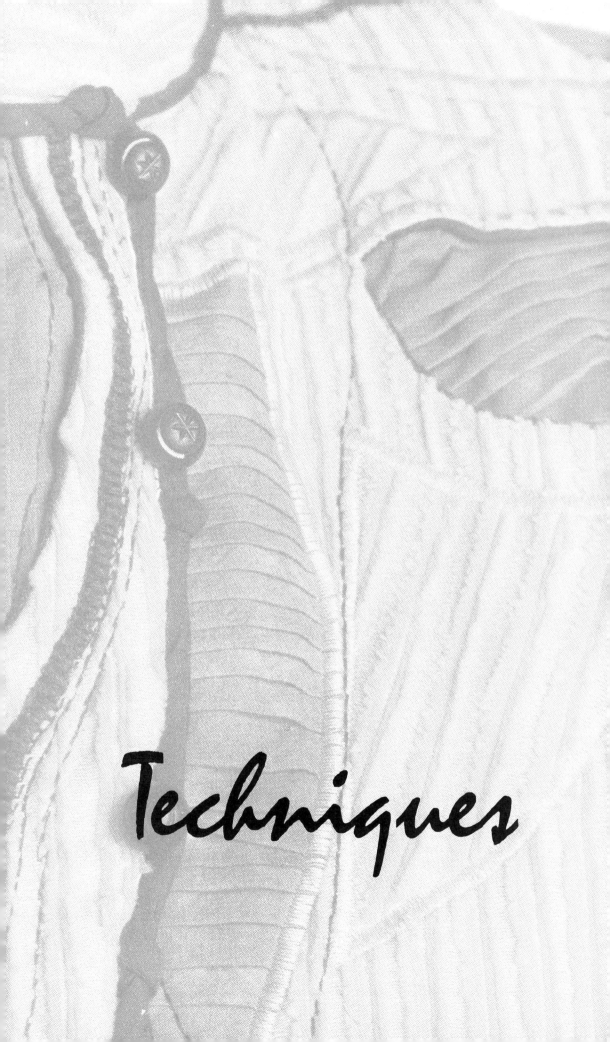

Techniques

Techniques

STITCHING
QUILTING
LEATHER LACING
PIPING
TUBES
TUCKS
PLEATS
TUNNELS
WRINKLED & STITCHED
FACED SHAPES
SHEERS
PIECING
GRIDS
BEADING & TRIMS

The techniques in this chapter present the basic methods. Added to this, is new input to stimulate a curiosity to experiment further. Your interpretation and design skills will combine to give your garment or other project your personal signature.

Texture is usually thought of as something visual. The best way to create a texture is to experiment with all the techniques you already know and combine them in a new way.

STITCHING

Machine stitching is by far the easiest, most satisfying method of enhancing your design. For those reluctant to trust their own design skills, this technique is a guaranteed confidence builder.

Stitching is best accomplished when the garment pieces are flat, possibly joined only at the shoulder seams. Using a double or triple needle with different shades of thread can give the appearance of multiple tucks. Stitching over lightweight batting or flannel will give a quilted look and extra firmness to the garment. This might be the perfect treatment for a collar, cuffs, sleeves or other sections of the garment. So many varieties of thread are available now. Metallic threads have been greatly improved, so they are a joy to use. Many rows of stitching are a great way to finish the edges of an elegant garment.

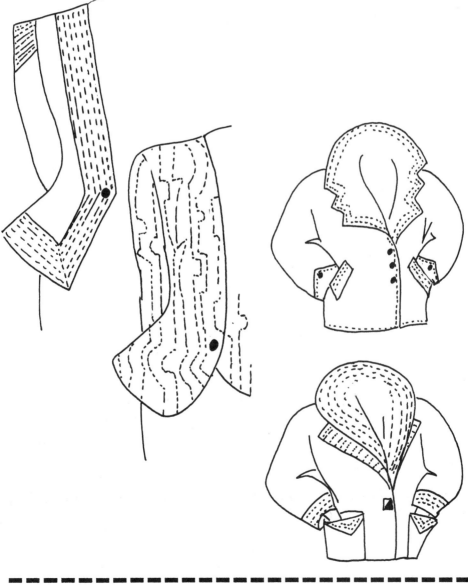

STITCHING, cont.

Cut shapes out of batting and place between the fashion fabric and an underlining. The shapes can be figures, trees, or abstract designs. Pin or baste around the shapes thru all thicknesses. Stitch around the shapes leaving the batting shapes free of stitching. Many rows of stitching accentuate the design. Consider combining satin stitching, in various widths, and straight stitching. *Note*: it is wise to cut the garment pieces an inch or two larger, then recut after stitching.

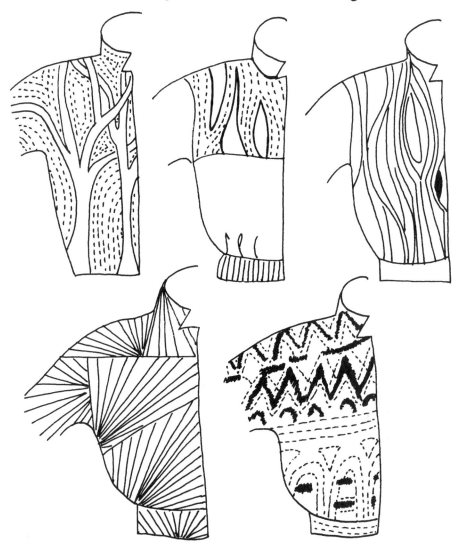

Another method to get a similar result would be to draw a design on an underlining fabric (or use a print as the underlining and follow the design on the print). Place a thin batting between the fashion fabric and the underlining. Pin and/or baste the three layers together. Sew from the underlining side so the design is visible. Solid stitching in the negative areas, leaves the design on the positive area rounded. This technique is very time consuming but well worth it. I have also seen it used on garment weight leather. Beautiful!

STITCHING, cont.

Stitching that looks like 'hatching' on a drawing certainly deserves some experimenting. One method would be to overlap cut organza shapes to create a landscape or other design. The edges of the organza would not necessarily need to be finished. Of course, the garment pieces could be cut out first and the design placed directly on the fashion fabric. When all the pieces are pinned in place, start stitching.

Another possibility would be appliqued pieces enhanced by stitching. All the stitching will eliminate the need to finish the edges. A design can also be achieved primarily by the stitching lines. The color of the thread and the density will create the visual impact.

QUILTING

Basically the technique of quilting is putting three layers together -- an underlining, the batting and the top. These layers are then stitched or somehow fastened together. I prefer machine stitching. There are several companies that make thin batting materials just for clothing. I would recommend them since practically no one needs or wants to look like a teddy bear in her jacket or coat.

There are probably more books written about quilting than any other sewing related subject. It would be very presumptuous of me to pass myself off as an expert on quilting. However, I would like to offer some ideas that might be new for you.

Quilted garments are very often made with cotton fabric and are fairly casual. Consider the unusual when making a fabric choice. This kind of thinking keeps your work fresh and new. Choose some silk crepe-de-chine for that baseball jacket and trim it with satin. Why not? Thin corduroy or other fabric with a nap would also be a good choice. Garment weight leather is simply wonderful when quilted. Knits can also be quilted. *Suggestion*: to keep knits from stretching, baste in a grid before machine quilting.

If part of the garment is to be textured or manipulated and the other part left plain, the plain areas need additional weight. Light batting added to untextured areas is one solution to give balance.

If quilting a whole garment is overwhelming, consider using some small contrasting quilted sections. The design on the main fabric selection might be the design on the quilted section as well.

QUILTING, cont.

The design and arrangement of the quilting lines is an opportunity to break away from the usual pattern of the stitching lines. Consider looking thru books, especially art books and various magazines for lines -- just lines -- in pleasing repetititions.

Suggestions:
      line drawings
      tire treads
      Japanese crests
      wallpaper borders
      art deco designs
      art nouveau flower shapes
and the list goes on...unlimited possibilites

Linda's
quilted
jacket

Be alert for fresh ideas. Always have a notebook handy to record images and artistic impressions.

LEATHER LACING

Punching and lacing a collar or jacket edge is a great way to finish leather, adding interest and a new texture. Leather lacing can also be used as an edge finish for fabric garments.

Note: Some advance planning is helpful. Choose a loosely woven fabric that will allow the threads to be eased apart for easy passage of the needle and strip.

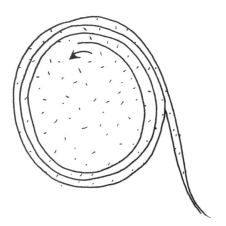

To make leather lacing: Use garment weight leather, cut a spiral as shown. A small 6"-8" piece of leather, will yield *yards* of 1/4" wide continuous strip.

In the case of a collar, shorten the interfacing at the outside edge, so that the leather will be passing thru the looser woven fabric and not distorting the finer weave of the interfacing fabric.

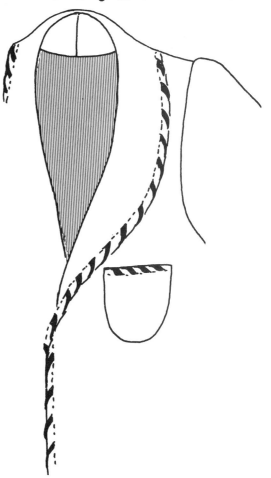

Using a large, blunt end tapestry needle, whipstitch the finished collar edge.

Take care to keep the leather strip flat, not twisted.

Press finished edge, using a pressing cloth and a clapper to 'set' the stitches.

Make a sample swatch to test your fabric and the stitches, varying the intervals to please yourself.

Collars, cuffs or pocket flaps are also possibilities for using this couture detailing idea, in addition to the jacket edges.

Linda contributed this great idea.

Linda's Wool Jacket
with Leather Lacing

PIPING

Corded piping adds a tailored accent to your garments. It's easy to make in a matching, contrasting or printed fabric.

Cut the bias strips 1 1//2" - 2" wide. I find it easier to handle, if it is wide. This accomodates most cording that will be covered. If the cording is very large, measure and plan accordingly. Available in various sizes, cotton cording can be purchased at most fabric stores. Linda suggests seine twine (#18) from the hardware store for a very narrow piping. Don't pre-shrink, just make sure the cording is slightly shorter than the bias so it isn't included in the crossing seams.

Fold the bias over the cording, right side out. Leave one side slightly narrower than the other to eliminate extra bulk in the seams. Stitch close to the cord using a zipper foot.

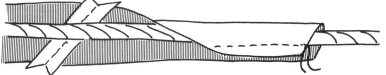

To add interest to your piping, strips of fabric, ribbon or leather can be applied. Fold over the piping, as shown. Pin and stitch.

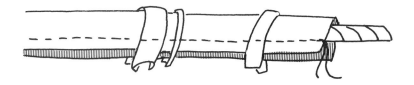

Lacing the piping with embroidery thread or pearl cotton adds an unexpected detail.

In addition to using cording, plastic beads on the continuous string are a possibility. They are usually available in fabric and craft stores.

I've also used zipper teeth, as a substitute for piping, on some very casual garments.

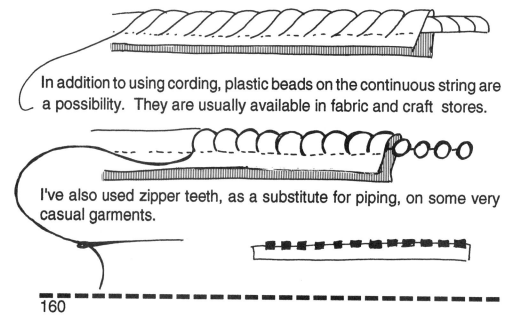

PIPING, cont.

To apply piping to the garment, pin the cording to the edge of the fabric at the seam allowance and stitch using the zipper foot. Stitch from the bias side, so the stitching line can be the guide. Place the companion piece of the garment together. Pin in place, right sides together. Stitch thru all thicknesses, using the previous stitching as a guide. Stitching just to the inside of the first stitching line is recommended to make a tight cording. Also clip the curves as needed.

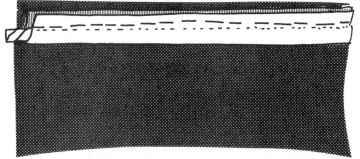

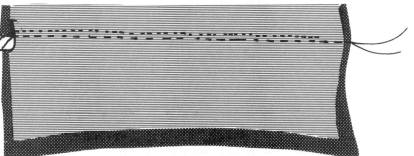

close-up of Linda's jacket shows piping inserted in seams

TUBES

Fabric tubes are easy to make and versatile in their use. They can be woven, applied to cover unfinished edges or emphasize a design element. Various widths used together can be interesting and can keep the project from being monotonous. Symmetry is not particularly my goal , so I don't measure the width of each strip. I cut the striped fabric lengthwise, crosswise or on the bias to give me the direction I need. If curves are needed I cut the strips on the bias. Most often my strips are 1 1/2" - 3" wide. For production sewing I stitch as shown and cut the stitching apart.

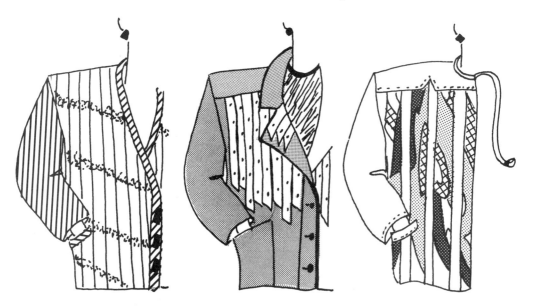

Turn the strips inside out if finished edges are important. If not, have the right side *out,* sew and press open with the seam in the middle of the strip. Unless it's important that the back is finished, it is unnecessary to turn the tubes.

Cut the strips of fabric as long as possible, especially if they are not to be turned inside out. Press flat. If the stripes are turned inside out, the seam can be on the side or in the middle, as preferred.

If the strips are to be applied, they can be stitched to the fashion fabric at 4"- 6" intervals or left loose, if that is practical. The fabric for the tubes could also be pieced before sewing into the tube shapes. This idea would be great if some color movement needs to be worked into the design. The examples show strips held by diagonal stitching, buttons or beads, or spacing to show the background fabric.

TUBES, cont.

If weaving, use a background fabric similar in color to the strips. Pin the lengthwise strips in place, To weave across, pin a strip horizontally in place. Move it across the vertical strips placing it over and under. Pin at the end of the row. Continue with this sequence alternating rows of weaving until the space is covered with woven strips. The weaving can combine other materials with the fabric strips, i.e. leather or Ultrasuede strips, ribbon, flat cording or braids, fancy knitting yarns.

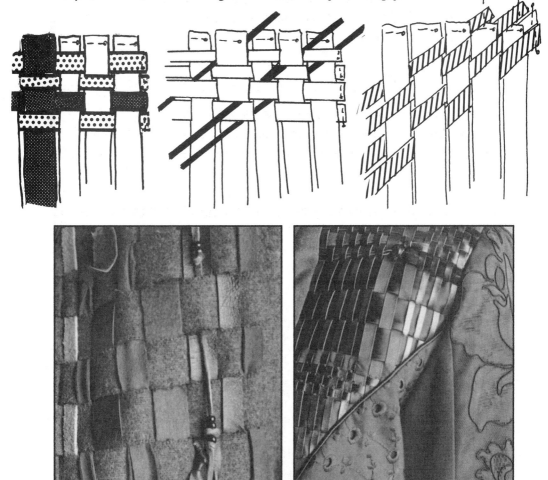

Grey flannel is slashed and woven with self fabric, leather & twisted cord with beads & coins.
Both examples are by Linda

This collage jacket is strip woven with leather, satin cord. Inset piping and lace overlays make it elegant.

TUBES, cont.

Wide tubes, some folded and some flat, can be applied as layers on a jacket. One edge would be stitched to a base fabric, the lower edge would be left open. If the first one applied is at the hem, consider creating an interesting hemline with that strip.

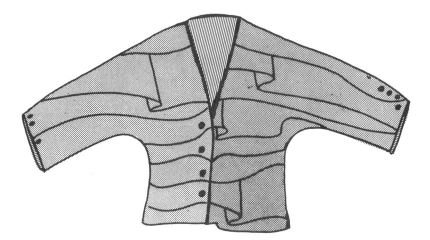

If the strips are bias, consider applying in curves by machine or hand-stitching in place. To secure, pin in the desired shape as shown. These can also be used to cover the unfinished edges of cut shapes. If the curves are 'tight' the pinned bias strips may need to be steamed to fit the spaces.

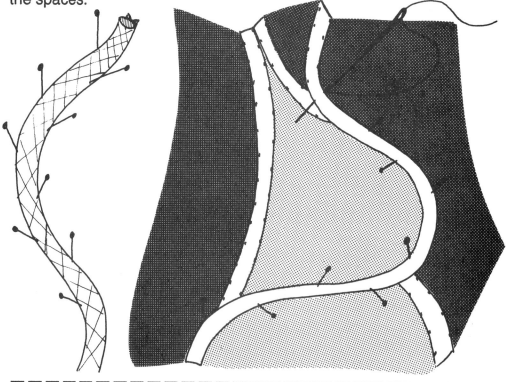

TUBES, cont.

This ribbed cotton jacket has bias tubes of black and white cotton handstitched in place, to look like highway stripes. The ravelled wool sections are machine stitched in place. Two Art Deco era buttons fasten with cording.

TUCKS

Something as utilitarian sounding as a tuck can also be a texture with great versatility. I have stitched and manipulated most tucks using striped fabric because I like the optical movement that occurs. The bonus for choosing stripes is that there are lines to follow as the tucks are stitched.

Finding the ' right' stripe is the first thing to do. Choose one that has a definite repetition in a reoccuring sequence. If there is some contrast in the color between the stripes, to whatever the degree, optical changes will be created. The more contrast in the colored stripes, the more conspicuous. As the garment moves on the body the colors seem to change before your eyes.

A 2 to 1 ratio in the width in the stripes works best. (One stripe might be 1/2" to 1" for the other stripe.) Decide now where to stitch the tucks. To do this, fold the stripe on the edge of one color. Bring the edge of this color to the next stripe of the same color. The resulting fold (A) is going to be the stitching line. Pin on that fold. The pin placement and the stitching line coincide.

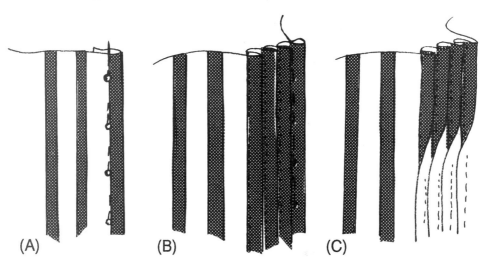

(A)   (B)   (C)

This tuck when folded back shows the 'other' color. No need to iron each one, simply fold and stitch the length of fabric desired. (B) The stripes will be a helpful guide. When the stitching is complete, press the tucks from one side with all one color showing. Press a section the width of the fabric. Then press the next section the opposite way to show the other color. (C) This gives an approximate direction showing how the 'waves' of color will appear. The directions of the stripes can be changed by ironing, when the pattern is placed on the fabric.
Note: I usually stitch my yardage and then figure out how creatively I can cut it.

TUCKS, cont.

TUCKS, cont.

Tucks can be sewn on plain or low-key prints. Tucking would be un-necessary if the fabric has a busy print. This detailing wouldn't show up enough to make doing this technique worthwhile. When a plain fabric is tucked, the texture is very pronounced. To me, it isn't important that the tucks be of equal width or distance from each other so I don't measure - or pin or baste. I fold and stitch the tucks in place and find it more interesting if the rows aren't perfect.

If the fabric is plain consider stitching the tucks with a decorative stitch. The stitching will show as the tucks are folded back and forth. If a decorative stitch is not possible, use a satin stitch in various widths.

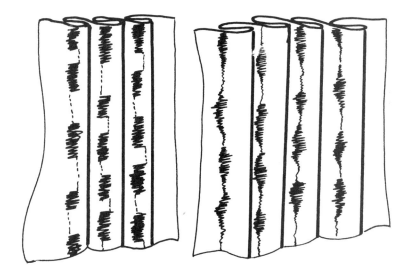

As the tucks are being sewn, add ribbon or folded fabric as inserts to make a particular design.

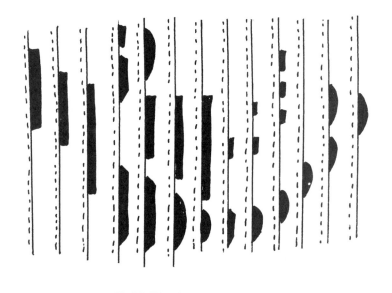

TUCKS, cont.

If the fabric is tucked, then the pattern cut, the bonus is the scraps that are left-over. These pieces can be used as inserts or combined with piecing or other techniques. *Note*: it's more challenging and creative, I think, to use the scraps 'as is', without re-cutting them. The vest pictured below, was made from the scraps from a jacket made for a magazine article. I used the faced shape technique to finish the edges. The buttons were an absolutely perfect match, they look like they've also been tucked. Serendipity!

Note: Some of the garments and comments on Tucks appeared in the Feb./Mar. 1992 issue of THREADS magazine.

PLEATS

Pleats have the same general look as the tuck, except the pleats are not stitched in place. One big plus for pleating the fabric before cutting the pattern is to eliminate the tedious marking of the pleats. Also you are free to use any pattern you wish, and place the pleats where desired. The easiest method to obtain pleats, aside from commercially pleated fabric, is to use a cloth pleater board (see suppliers).

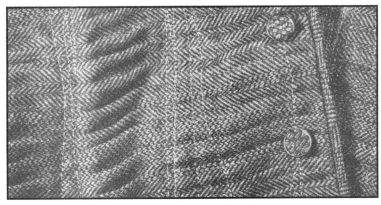

Here are a few suggestions that may help you when using this wonderful device. To use the pleater, place on the ironing board with the open louvers away from you. Tuck the fabric into the louvers with your fingers (some like to use a plastic ruler or credit card), being careful to push the fabric in all the way. I place the fabric wrong side up. Lightweight iron-on interfacing, either a narrow strip on each end or a piece covering the entire surface, keeps the pleats together. Cut the interfacing slightly smaller than the pleated piece to keep from bonding to the pleater. Using a pressing cloth, iron with the warmest setting appropriate for the fabric. Let cool before gently removing from the pleater. Roll the pleater back and the fabric simply falls out....no need to pull it. To keep the pleater in perfect condition, iron it when you are finished, in case it has been dampened.

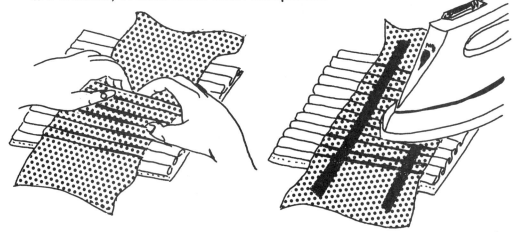

Note: the pleats made in this way are not intended to be used for pleated skirts.

PLEATS, cont.

The pleated fabric is now ready to use. The fabric chosen will determine how permanent these pleats will be. Most often the pleats will have to be held in place by some additional means.

On this black and white silk suit jacket, I have pleated the fabric and then cut it as per my pattern. The pleats are sewn horizontally by machine, then the cording is applied by hand. The cording is wrapped to make the buttonholes where appropriate. The buttons are silver beads.

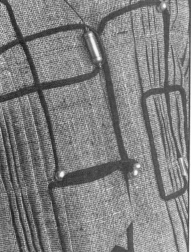

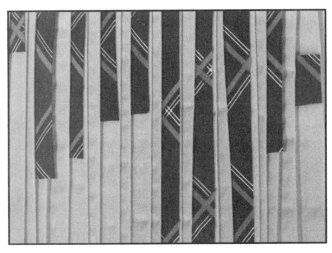

bias tape inserted in pleats

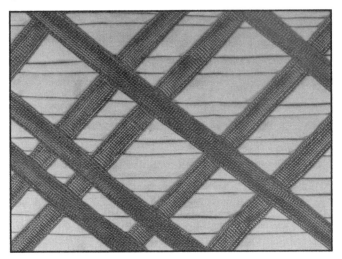

braid sewn to hold pleats in place

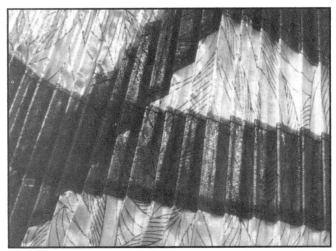

sheer strips sewn to metallic fabric before pleating

PLEATS, cont.

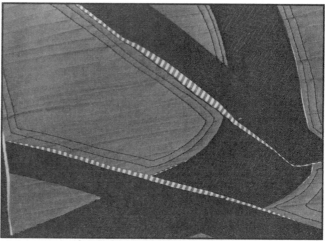

faced shapes to hold pleats in place

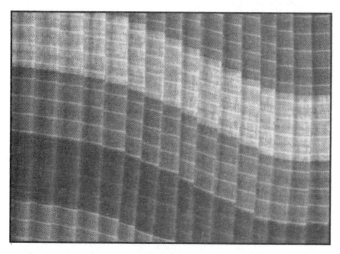

stripes maneuvered into a wave design

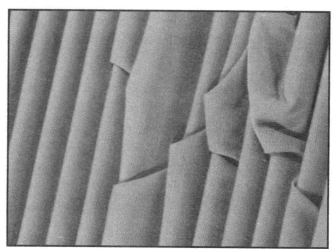

fabric folded before pleating

TUNNELS

In my experiments to create texture, I wanted to manipulate fabric to look like curved tucks. Sewing tucks didn't work well, so I devised a way to make tunnels of fabric that could have rounded, curvy lines.

The fashion fabric that works best is one that has some body -- such as wool...most any kind. Melton is one of my favorites. Menswear suiting is good, heavy cottons or silks work well. It is best to try a sample if the fabric is soft, maybe an iron-on interfacing would be a solution.

The fashion fabric will be stitched to an underlining material -- muslin, sheeting or other 'uglies' that need to be used up.

The whole concept is that the top layer will be stitched to the bottom layer starting at one side. The top layer is picked up and moved over to create the tunnel of fabric. It is then pinned and stitched in place. If the stitching lines are curved the tunnels will also follow that line. There can be flat spaces between the tunnels with many rows of stitching, if desired. The tunnels can be large, small, stuffed. Covered cording or flat trims could also be added on top of the tunnels to enhance and exaggerate the lines.

This technique definitely adds stability to the fabric. Use that quality to advantage. Consider piecing the fabric before tunnelling or cutting up the tunnelled fabric to make a collage.

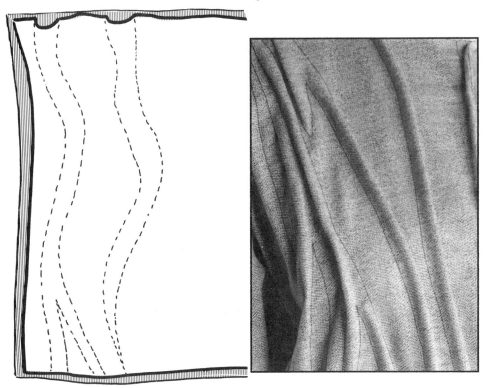

TUNNELS, cont.

Grey menswear suiting is the fabric chosen for this tunnelled jacket. The closure is made of corded loops ending with wrapping. Bias bands finish the edges.

Wool and silk blend in winter white with black slubs is the fashion fabric for this short banded jacket. The tunnels are a much smaller scale than the other example. The closure is part of a bracelet. Some of the links of the bracelet (see detail) have been incorporated with the covered cording as surface decoration.

WRINKLED & STITCHED

Wrinkling and twisting a fabric made of natural fibers can create a wonderful texture. China silk is one of my favorites;on the photo below I have applied the silk to wool boucle. The pocket is Ultrasuede.

Method:
Dampen the fabric, then twist it very tightly until it curls up on itself. Tie the twisted fabric into several knots. Dry in the dryer, if possible or let air dry. Keep it tied for a few days to set the wrinkles. If larger folds of fabric are needed, fold or accordian pleat and secure with rubber bands or tie firmly.

If I am creating large pieces of 'yardage' I place the twisted fabric on top of an underlining material. If only a small area is to be covered with the twisted fabric, it is placed directly on the fashion fabric.

When the wrinkled/twisted fabric is dry, it is pinned to the underlining or other fabric as desired. The wrinkles are set in an already established pattern, so spread the fabric and pin and/or baste to keep in place.Working from one side to the other, stitch the two layers together. Now machine stitch along the wrinkles. Stitch as needed letting the stitching outline the shapes of the wrinkles.

WRINKLED & STITCHED, cont.

You may wish to use contrasting thread to make the stitching more important. Or use a double needle, perhaps, in two nearly matching shades of thread. If free motion embroidery is one of your skills, this is a great technique to use. Corded piping, ribbon, or other bits of fabric can be added where the wrinkles are large enough to cover the unfinished edges.

Horizontal or diagonal rows of ribbon, bias tubes or strips of Ultrasuede, 4"-5" apart, can be stitched to keep the wrinkles in place. This alternative method works very well.

FACED SHAPES

In sewing, I am looking for a certain effect to create an illusion. When I want the look of applique without all the tedious handwork, I use a technique that I call faced shapes. Facings have always been considered a utilitarian necessity, one that finishes the edges of a cuff, collar or front opening. That is one possibility .... read on.

I have used this technique more than any other in past years. It seems to be a great design feature, and a wonderful way to solve many sewing 'problems'. Ideas:
> • define an edge with a contrasting color or fabric
> • finish an unusual shape on collars, pockets, cuffs
> • make easy shaped buttonholes
> • create a shaped hemline

Various shapes can be faced and used as decorative details. These applied shapes can be positive (overlapping shapes or flaps) or negative (cut-out holes or 'windows'). The negative shapes could have textured or other special textile pieces placed in back of the 'hole'. This could also be a 'real' buttonhole or a shaped pocket opening.

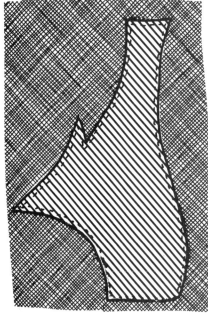 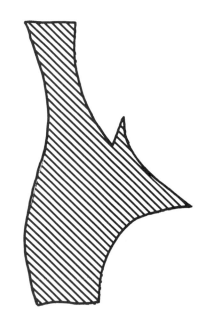

Method: I usually cut one piece the shape I wish, then place it on top of a piece slightly larger in the shape of a rectangle or square.This eliminates the chance of pulling the cut pieces out of shape and makes it easier to handle while sewing. Place right sides together and stitch. Trim & clip. Leave one section open for turn thru, or if all sides are finished, cut a small slit in the back of the facing and pull the shape to the right side. Press. These shapes can then be applied easily by machine stitching or tacking by hand.

The designs on the grey wool suit jacket look quite intricate. However the simple technique of the faced shapes was used. The facings were long strips of dark red wool placed on top of the jackets pieces. The shapes were stitched, then cut, trimmed and pressed to show a little of the red facing. A larger piece of plain grey wool was placed behind the finished hole and top stitched around thru all thicknesses.

FACED SHAPES, cont.

I use faced shapes in many ways not only to solve a particular construction problem, but also to create the design concept. To make this idea work well, I choose a shape that relates to some part of the garment, possibly the lapels or even the design on the buttons. The ideas, below, were inspired by buttons from my collection. The plan is to make a piece that looks like a cuff, in reality it is a faced piece of fabric... a flap that is merely set into the sleeve seam.

This flap is an exaggerated sized 'cuff', 6 - 8" at the widest part and long enough to start at the sleeve seam and wrap around to the front about at the wristbone. The length depends on the width of the sleeves so make a paper pattern or cut out a scrap of fabric to determine that measurement (probably about 15"). If this is a raglan or dolman sleeve the 'cuff' starts at the seam on the top so 7"- 8" for the length would suffice. The photographs on the opposite page and the third diagram below show the raglan sleeve insertion.

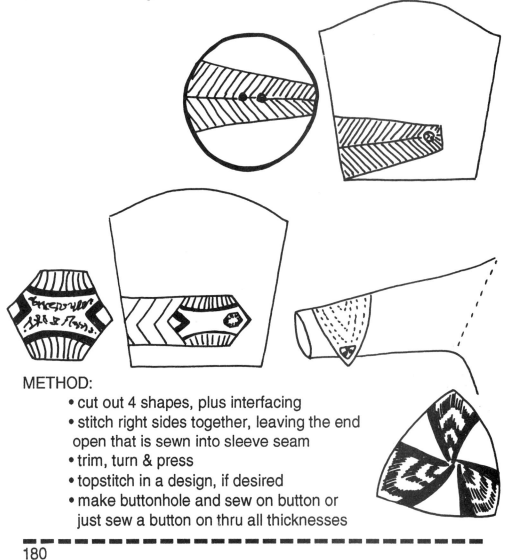

METHOD:
- cut out 4 shapes, plus interfacing
- stitch right sides together, leaving the end open that is sewn into sleeve seam
- trim, turn & press
- topstitch in a design, if desired
- make buttonhole and sew on button or just sew a button on thru all thicknesses

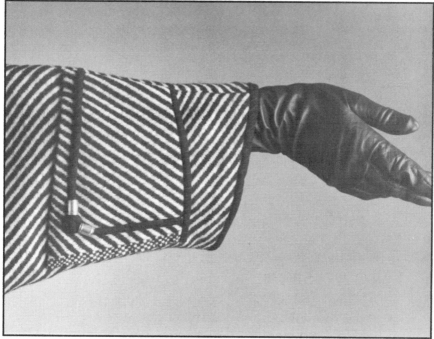

Black wool with cream lines is combined with a woven paisley. The faced shapes at the lower edge of the black is faced with taffeta. This extends the lines so they appear as tabs over the paisley. The placement of the black buttons on the design seems just right and not necessarily equal distance apart. The collar is cut of the paisley. The sleeves and lower hem are finished with black bias bands.

FACED SHAPES, cont.

If the shapes to be finished are simple ones, bias strips can be used. Striped fabric as the bias add an eye-catching detail. Cut the bias strips 1 1/2" or wider and stitch it to the edge to be faced. Clip, trim, turn & press. On the photo below, the white stripes on the bias almost appear as bright beads.

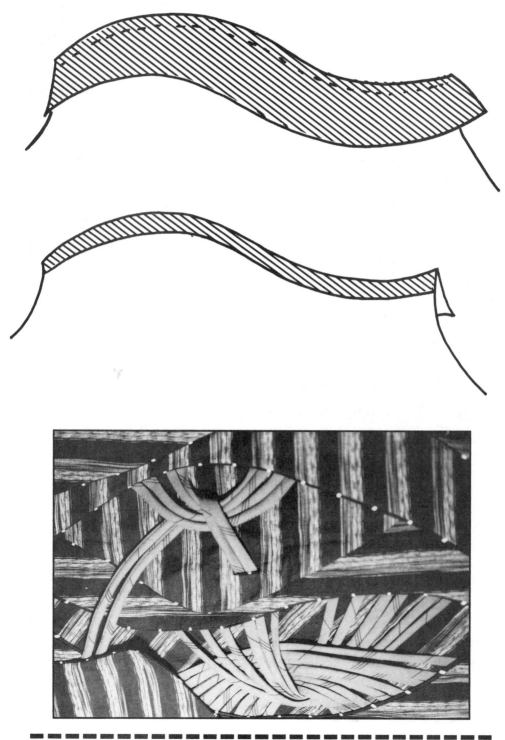

SHEERS

There could be several reasons for using fabric in layers. One would be to cover a less than desirable color. By placing a sheer fabric of another color on top, the color of the base fabric would change.

On the first close-up, I used some tapestry medallions from an old kimono. Both sides of the medallions were usable; in fact I liked the texture of the back side best so I used both sides. The background was navy blue. I wanted the navy to appear black. I applied the pieces to a black and grey striped taffeta and covered the entire vest with black organza. The sheer softened the striped taffeta and unified all sections of the garment. Silver metallic thread to match the buttons and a few silver beads completed the vest.

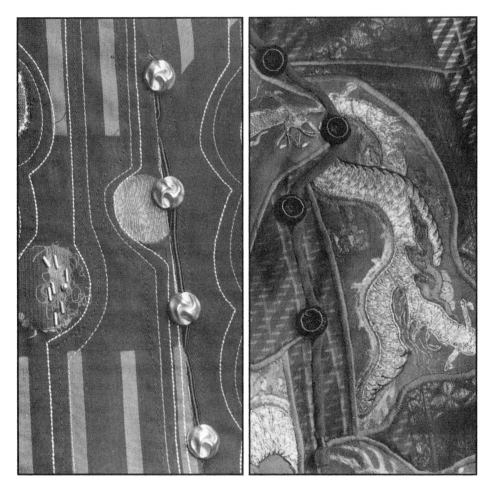

On the other photo, I have applied the metallic embroidery from an old Chinese dragon robe. The wide embroidered bands that coordinated so well seemed to be a bit too bright so I covered them with organza to center the attention on the dragons.

SHEERS, cont.

The two most common sheer fabrics to consider would be organza (rather stiff and sheer) and chiffon (very soft, drapey and sheer). Both fabrics are available in silk and polyester. The silk organza has a matt finish, the polyester has a sheen. Usually there is very little difference in the cost. Sheers are definitely fun to experiment with so the next time you are in the fabric store, visit the bridal/formal department.

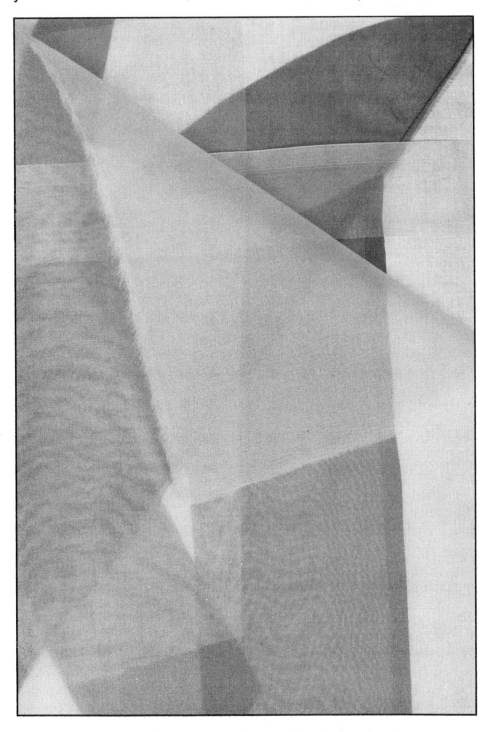

SHEERS, cont.

A sheer placed over any fabric will definitely change the color and/or value of the base fabric. The whole feeling of the piece changes. If the base fabric is striped, consider covering it with a sheer floral print. Another idea is to use two colors of sheer combined to make a third color.

Suggestion: Arrange shapes i.e. triangles or squares between two layers of organza. Stitch around each shape to keep them in place and emphasize those shapes. Another plus for using the sheer overlay is that the edges of the pieces underneath can be left unfinished.

This silk and wool jacket has printed appliques covered sporadically with black organza. Strands of pearl cotton are machine stitched in place. The garment is quilted for warmth

SHEERS, cont.

On this black and white vest I have used a sheer/solid fabric that is checkered in 3" squares. The textures underneath the sheer/solid seem distorted, it takes a moment to figure out what is going on there. I have combined some silk/linen tucked & manipulated pieces with some ikat cotton.

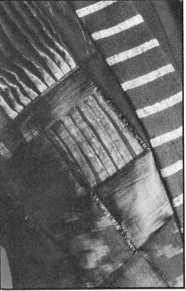

PIECING

Piecing or patchwork is a method used for putting sections of fabric together. Piecing can have versatile results. Be innovative, try a new approach on the next pieced project. Usually pieces are sewn, right sides together, with the seams pressed open. There are many other options. Prints can be cut up and re-sewn. If the print is 'busy' or boring divide the fabric into sections and sew a plain strip of fabric to separate the pieces. Numbering the sections is helpful if the order is important.

PIECING, cont.

Stripes placed in a definite design give visual optical impact. Consider appliqueing some irregular shapes on top to break-up the repetition.

Small scraps can be overlapped and topstitched, unfinished edges showing. I personally like the added texture of the ravelling.

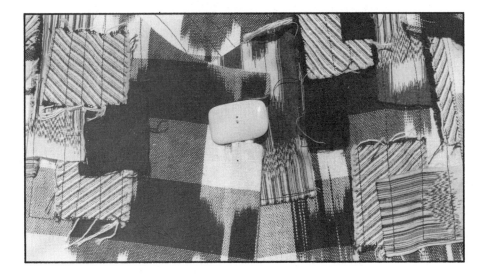

GRIDS

I like the dimensional look that can be achieved by making a network of lines. It is easy to apply the grid over any fabric.

The grid could be:
- a heavy netting with large openings
- a narrow braid, like soutache, applied on top of a texture or print, fastening the braid where the rows cross
- heavy stitching lines in a crossed design

Consider sewing beads or making knots at the grid intersections.

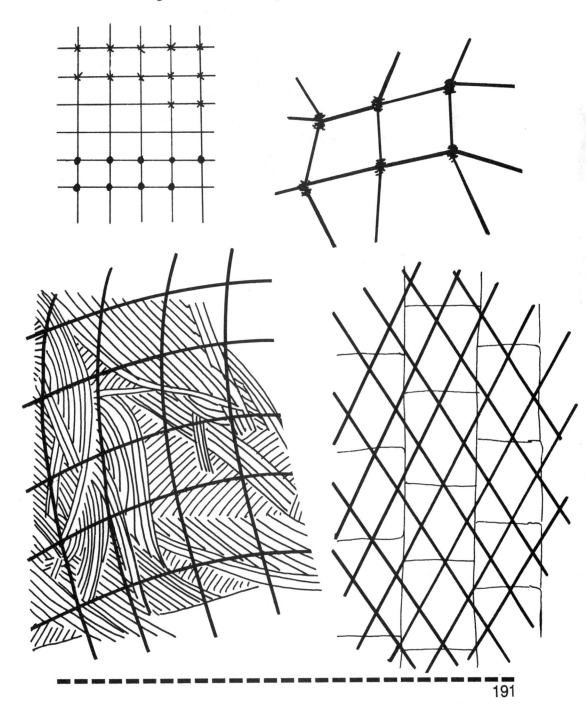

BEADING & TRIMS

Beading a large section of a garment can be time consuming and tedious. To speed the process, I start with some interesting braids or other trims that will be used with the beads. Logical focal points are the collar, cuffs, pockets. Consider the placement for visual impact. If a special design for the beading is desired, look in the library at various art books. Two suggestions would be books on stained glass designs or stencilling ideas. Also using the 'window' ideas from the first chapter is a great way to get an asymmetrical design.

I place and pin the braids, etc. on the garment pieces. It is easier to work on the pieces than the whole garment.

The beads and trims will be quite heavy so these areas need to be interfaced. I use tailor's felt, it keeps the pieces from 'sagging'. Tailor's felt can be obtained at tailor supply stores. Other suggestions for interfacing are hair canvas or other woven interfacing possibly combined with flannel. A quilted surface has enough stability without additional interfacing.

I usually apply the trims and braids by hand since I haven't found a satisfactory method by machine. Some people successfully use invisible thread with the blind hem stitch. You may wish to try that idea.

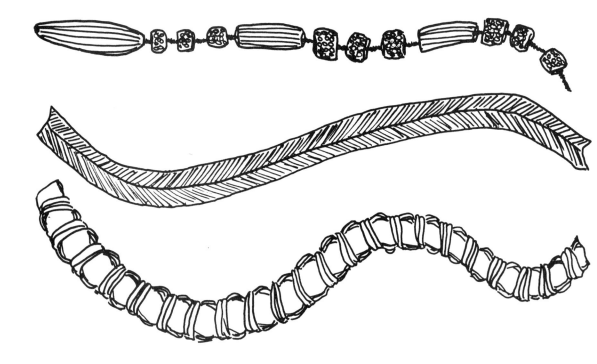

BEADING & TRIMS, cont.

Passementerie.... even the word is elegant. It encompasses all the various forms that trimming with braids, cords and beads can take. On the example below, the black ribbed wool jacket has applied pieces of something similar to battenberg lace. Piping at the edge of the yoke and black jet buttons add the finishing touches.

Metalic embroidered sari braid is applied to this asymmetrical collar. Narrow lame´piping is inserted on the edges of this black crepe batwing jacket by Linda.

After all the trims are in place, add the beads to fill in the design and add some pizazz. There is such a variety of beads to choose from. My two favorites are bugle beads... they are the narrow tubes and seed beads... those very small ones that the needle sometimes doesn't like to go thru. Everyone has ingenious ways of getting the beads on the needle. I find it easy to put the seed beads in a small dish and 'stab' the beads. They seem to jump on the needle.

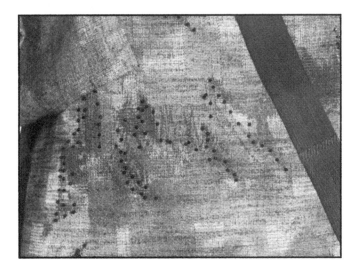

I take a back stitch after sewing on several beads to fasten securely. The thread I like is called waxon. It comes in a hank that is cut to dispense one thread at a time. (It can also be purchased at a tailor supply.) It is great for handsewing; never knots up.

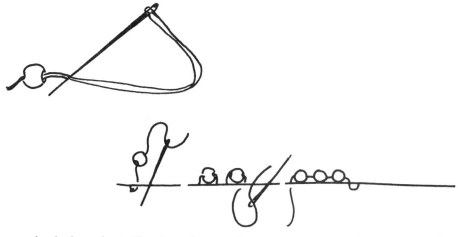

For a single bead application, fasten thread, come up thru the bead, then down into the fabric. Secure the stitches after every 2 or 3 beads by backstitching. Small round beads can also be sewn on in groups by placing several on a thread and sewing 2 or 3 at a time.

The stop bead application requires 2 beads, one large and one small. For example, a seed bead on top to hold the larger flat one in place.

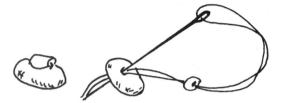

As with other beads there are many ways to apply them and bugle beads are no exception. They can be sewn on flat, as shown below or upright with a small round bead on the end. These are my favorite kind of beads to use as a fill-in. They come in various lengths and take up a lot of space.

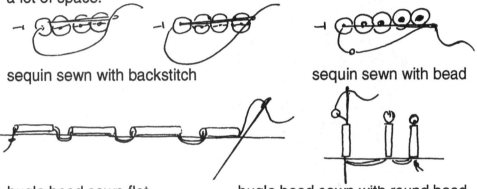

sequin sewn with backstitch   sequin sewn with bead

bugle bead sewn flat   bugle bead sewn with round bead

Sequins add a lot of sparkle and the clear ones are more 'low-key' if that is a consideration. I recently saw some plaid fabric that was covered with clear sequins. The same plaid without the sequins was sold as a companion piece. It was unexpectedly wonderful!

To combine quilting with beading:
    a. fasten with back stitch, stitch thru all layers
    b. back thru bead
    c. take a stitch thru all layers and place needle for next
       application

Beading can add sparkle to a rather casual garment, see page 184. At the other extreme, it can be very elegant with trims and beads lavishly applied.

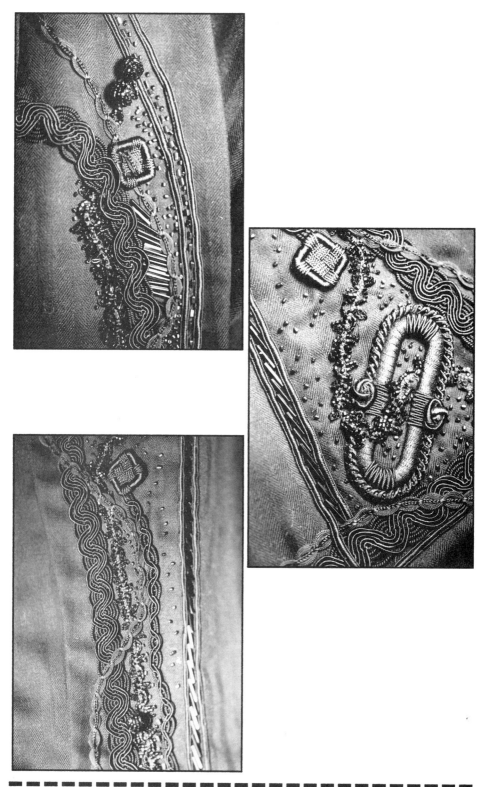

BEADING & TRIMS, cont.

If the collar, or other beaded section needs pressing, place wrong side up on a terry cloth towel and use a pressing cloth. The fabrics I have used successfully for the pieces I have beaded are menswear suiting or other wools, cotton tapestry, heavy silks. If underlined properly or quilted, most any fabric would probably work well. When small areas are beaded solidly, an embroidery hoop or a scroll frame are advantageous.

If a beaded shape is to be applied to a garment as an applique, the beading can be done on organza. When finished, glue the back of the beaded piece; when dry cut-out the shape. *Note:* Choose a glue that dries clear. Glue the cut edges, to keep from ravelling. Apply the beaded applique to a garment where desired by handstitching in place.

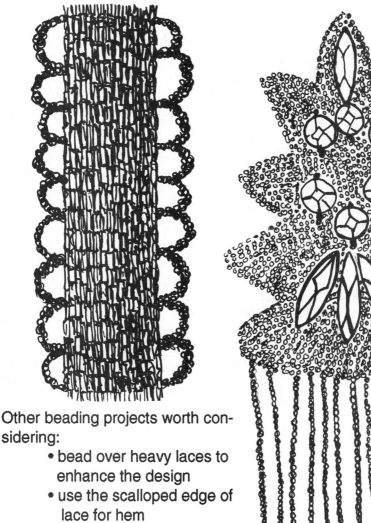

Other beading projects worth considering:
- bead over heavy laces to enhance the design
- use the scalloped edge of lace for hem
- bead the border of a print that has been quilted
- bead a paisley

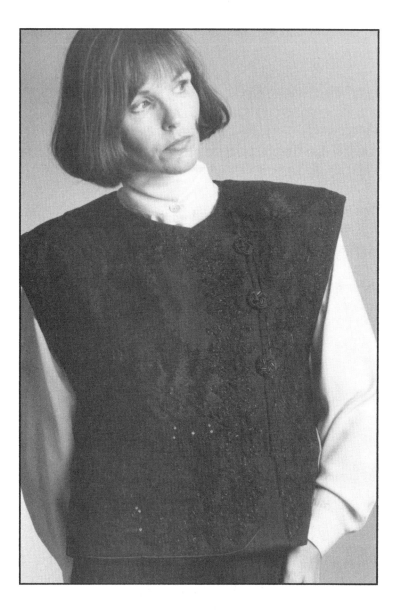

BEADING & TRIMS

I've collected jet beaded fabrics for many years. Some were insets on dresses, collars, border or trims. All were handbeaded in an era when handwork of this kind was affordable. At the turn of the century, women worked 84 hours a week for $10.!!! Many of the pieces I have are from the l920's and 30's.

To use these wonderful beaded pieces, I have made a collage of them and applied the pieces to a black silk faille. I have underlined the faille with tailor's felt (see suppliers). All these pieces were quite heavy so I wanted to make sure they were well stabilized.

The beaded pieces were arranged on the faille and handstitched in place. The three collars that I had were not, of course, used at the neck. They were applied at the armholes and at the front opening. The beading was fragile in several places so the whole vest was covered with two layers of nylon net. I first tried silk organza but it obscured the beads. The netting was hand-stitched, to keep all three layers together.

A shimmering lavender lining finishes the inside. The corded buttonhole at the asymmetrical closing were applied, with old jet buttons as the finale'.

Bibliography

Beaney, Jan: ART OF THE NEEDLE, Pantheon Books, N.Y. 1988

Bowman, Sara: A FASHION FOR EXTRAVAGANCE, E.P.Dutton, N.Y., 1985

Croner, Marjorie: FABRIC PHOTOS, Interweave Press, Colo., 1989

Edwards, Betty: DRAWING ON THE ARTIST WITHIN, Simon and Shuster, N.Y., 1986

Franck, Frederick: ART AS A WAY, Crossroad, N.Y., 1981

Gostelow, Mary, THE COMPLETE GUIDE TO NEEDLEWORK, Chartwell Books, N.J. , 1984

Marshall, John: MAKE YOUR OWN JAPANESE CLOTHES, Kodansha International, Tokyo & N.Y., 1988

Miyake, Issey: ISSEY MIYAKE, Irving Penn (Photos), Little, Brown & Co., Boston, Toronto, London, 1988

Moore, Nancy: MACHINE QUILTED JACKETS, VESTS AND COATS Chilton Book Co., Pa., 1991

Smith, Barbara Lee: CELEBRATING THE STITCH, Taunton Press, Ct. 1991

Thompson, Angela: EMBROIDERY WITH BEADS, Batsford Books, London, 1990

Suppliers

BEADS, THREADS:

Aardvark, Box 2449, Livermore,Ca. 94550 (800) 388-ANTS
Beads - Beads, 949 N. Tustin Ave. Orange,Ca. (714) 639-1611
Shipwreck Beads, 5021 Mud Bay Rd., Olympia, Wa. 98502

FABRIC PAINT: (non-toxic)
Createx,14Airport Park Rd. East Granby, Ct. 06026 (800) 243-2712

FASTURN:
The Crowning Touch, 2410 Glory C Rd., Medford, Or. 97501
        (503) 772-8430

LACE, VINTAGE 'TREASURES'
Lacis, 2982 Adeline St., Berkeley, Ca. 04703 (415) 843-7178

NOTIONS:
Nancy's Notions, Box 683, Beaver Dam, Wi. 53916 (414) 887-0690

PLEATERS AND BOOKS:
Lois Ericson, Box 5222, Salem, Or. 97304

TAILORS SUPPLY:
Oregon Tailor Supply, 2123 S.E. Division St., Portland, Or.
        (800) 678-2457
Most large cities have a tailor's supply, so check the yellow pages.

Index

Guest Author

I specialize in contemporary couture. I thrive on meticulously executed details and inventive construction. Designing offers constant challenges with new techniques; to interpret details that I have seen or imagined. Teaching gives me the enjoyment of guiding others toward a level of self-confidence and proficiency that allows the freedom of design with ability to execute the idea into a truly professional look and wearable art garment. If you call this work -- then I love my job!

Linda Wakefield
237 N. Pine St.
Orange, Ca. 92666

As a designer, I want to create something unique.
As a teacher, I encourage others to observe the art
    that exists in their world.
As a person, I want to connect with those who
    share the same love of sewing.

Lois Ericson
P.O. Box 5222
Salem, Or. 97304

BOOKS BY LOIS ERICSON:

SHAPED WEAVING*
THE BAG BOOK*
ETHNIC COSTUME*
PRINT IT YOURSELF
    (WITH DIANE ERICSON)
DESIGN & SEW IT YOURSELF
    (WITH DIANE ERICSON)
BELTS...WAISTED SCULPTURE*
FABRICS....RECONSTRUCTED
TEXTURE...a closer look
PLEATS

* out of print

"WHAT I AM IS A BODY ATTACHED TO A PAIR OF HANDS THAT CAN'T STOP MAKING THINGS"

.... anonymous